Never-ending Love

Never-ending Love

Sharing Stories, Prayers and **Comfort** for **Miscarriage** and **Infant Loss**

Edited by **Anne Louise Mahoney**

TWENTY-THIRD PUBLICATIONS
twentythirdpublications.com

Twenty-Third Publications
977 Hartford Turnpike Unit A • Waterford, CT 06385
(860) 437-3012 or (800) 321-0411 • twentythirdpublications.com

Cover design: Jeff McCall
Cover image: 60seconds/stock.adobe.com

ISBN: 978-1-62785-774-1

Published in Canada by Novalis

Cover design and layout: Audrey Wells
Cover image: iStock/anyaberkut

Publishing Office
1 Eglinton Avenue East, Suite 800
Toronto, Ontario, Canada
M4P 3A1

Head Office
4475 Frontenac Street
Montréal, Québec, Canada
H2H 2S2

en.novalis.ca

Cataloguing in Publication is available from Library and Archives Canada.
ISBN: 978-2-89688-900-6

Printed in Canada.

bayard A division of Bayard, Inc.

Contents

"I have loved you with an everlasting love…"

Jeremiah 31:3

Introduction

"I just don't know what to say or do."

So often, in the face of suffering, we find ourselves doing or saying nothing out of fear of making things worse. The chapters of this book are a confirmation that for many people experiencing miscarriage and infant loss, the absence and silence actually contribute to and worsen the pain of loss.

Thankfully, there are many things we can prayerfully consider as a response to the grief of parents and families, individually and in our communities of faith. Reading this book is a wonderful step on the personal and collective journey toward our church and our world being a safer place for this particular kind of grief.

Maybe the most significant thing we can do is normalize being and becoming a safe space for people to share the stories of their losses. These pages hold the sacred stories of lives that existed only briefly on this side of heaven, told lovingly by the parents with aching arms and souls. Practise listening with an open heart. Read with reverence. Pay attention to unique ways that each of these writers experienced their loss, waded through it and made meaning. Watch for the people who were walking alongside. You'll learn in these pages that there is no one right way to respond, but there are many ways to respectfully make yourself available, offer support and be a part of a healing journey.

Because miscarriage is such a profoundly interior and hidden loss, I invite you to begin by reflecting on your own connection to this subject. Have you experienced a loss of your own? A child, niece, nephew, grandchild or close friend? Have you had a difficult situation in trying to give support and feeling like it didn't go well? Have you walked alongside someone and asked what more you could do? Pull out a journal or go for a walk and reflect on your reason for caring. Are there any wounds that God may want to heal in you? Doing this healing work of your own first will allow you to enter into others' pain with less likelihood that your motives will intrude on their grief. May the pages that follow be a part of your healing, too.

As you read, take note of the many things individuals have said and done that the writers have found helpful. Write them down so you can refer back when you're preparing to connect with a family after a loss. Pray over the choices and ask God to direct you to the one most needed in the moment. Trust that saying or doing something with empathy and humility is better than doing or saying nothing at all. Apologize and try again if needed. When offering practical supports, remember that generalized offers of help put the responsibility on the grieving to call and ask, which can be overwhelming and exhausting. Offer specific supports that you are able to follow through on and give the other person permission to accept or decline without shame.

Communal responses are also a powerful part of changing the culture of silent isolation. When our churches have posters up in hallways and bathrooms, brochures advertising options for support at the entrances, services advertised and offered regularly, and prayers of the faithful for miscarried children and their families, we make the whole community more aware of the frequency of these losses and the supports available. Consider being a part of efforts in your church and/or diocese as well as your broader community to strengthen and sustain miscarriage resources and ministry.

Finally, I invite you to pay attention to the seasons of grieving as articulated by the stories in this collection. The hope and possibility and uncertainty of pregnancy. The loss. Grief and confusion and doubt. An embodied path to healing and a God big enough to hold the pain. The role of ritual and spiritual practices in gradual healing. The power of sharing. It is impossible to know where people are at, how they are feeling or what they need without asking them. May these pages give you courage and hope that reaching out to ask is always a gift, especially when those you are connecting with have the freedom to accept or decline support.

These writers have given their perspectives with such beauty and honesty and generosity from their own varied perspectives. May their words inspire your own journey of healing and hope for yourself and your community.

The little ones remembered in this book are part of a great communion of saints whose lives are almost entirely eternal. May they pray with us and for us for a world that never takes for granted the miracle of a single life and grieves well the ones we haven't gotten to hold.

Leah Perrault
July 28, 2023

Part 1

Personal Stories

Gifts and Graces

Reflecting on Loss

Brenda Merk Hildebrand

For almost 20 years, the memory of our little one born too soon was a dark place of confusing pain, misunderstanding and loss. Most of the time, it was easy to live around this emptiness. Family, friends, work, community and parish commitments offered a life that was full and abundant. Three children came into our home, their presence a joy and a blessing. The all-too-short life of our little one, ending in a miscarriage, faded into the background. And yet, each year, on what would have been her birthday, I quietly remembered the child of my heart.

It seemed wise to carry on. It was wise, and good, to carry on. The world certainly did not want to dwell on this difficult loss. Women were to bear all losses quietly and move on quickly. There was no funeral, no memorial service, no formal acknowledgement of this life or this death; it simply did not fit into the usual categories of grief.

When the time was right, and I was ready, God invited me back to that place of darkness so it could be filled with light. Tearful, I dared to ask the questions that had long been unanswered: "You know, God, that all life has purpose and all life is sacred. Why did our little one have to be born too soon? What was her purpose? How did her life matter? What difference did she make?"

What I say to you in the darkness, speak in the light;
What you hear whispered, proclaim on the housetops.
(Matthew 10.27)

I waited, quietly attentive, while the answers came. Seen only by me, our little one had awakened in me a love for life and a willingness to protect it. I treasured more deeply the pregnancies, births and lives of our children. My work as a childbirth educator was deeply enriched. I was more sensitive to the joy and the pain that can accompany this life-changing transition. When my class of grade 6 and 7 Catholic students asked what I thought about the intrinsic value of all life, I could answer very clearly. As I write this, I wonder about the lasting effect that answer might still have, and I am chuckling because the question was posed when I was almost eight months pregnant with our next child.

Until this time of healing prayer, and the recollection of those events, almost 20 years after that difficult experience, I had not even been aware of the ways in which this little one had lived on in my life. It was time to honour her legacy.

It was time to give this little one a name. It was time to share the darkness and the light, beginning with my husband and our children. I still treasure my husband's sincere love as he looked at the baptismal gown that was worn by our other children. It was a symbol of what had been, to that point, an inward journey. I am grateful for his willingness to share that experience.

Recalling that at every Baptism, parents are asked to speak aloud the name they have chosen for their child, I asked if she could be named Amy Marie. Amy means "beloved," and I shared my belief that she was beloved and fully at home with God. I acknowledged the pain I felt at the Baptisms of each of our other children when I received the blessing given to a new mother. In those years, the blessing noted that the mother gave thanks to God for the gift of this child. All good. The next sentence asked the mother to give this child back to God. That was not as easy. I had already given one child back.

The healing process brought good news into my life. Yes, one child had been reluctantly given back. What I had not seen, until that time of prayer-filled healing, was that Amy Marie had been gently returned to me. I had been blind to the quiet blessings her life had offered. And in that time of quiet, the promise offered by St. Paul became real.

> We know that all things work together
> for good for those who love God,
> who are called according to his purpose.
> *(Romans 8.28)*

While this healing process was still fresh, a dear, sensitive and thoughtful friend offered two roses: one for me and one for Amy. One red and one white, they were held together with a ribbon, symbolizing that we are forever united. Our love is never-ending.

Throughout the healing process, I learned to re-view the past and to see it from a new perspective. The gift of this new perspective has allowed me to live more deeply in the present moment. I see and hear and perceive in a new way.

When people ask me how many children we have, I answer in the usual conventional manner: "We have three children."

Every once in a great while, something prompts me to say "four," following up with an acknowledgement of the little one who was born too soon.

On each of those occasions, the person with whom I am speaking has become quiet. After a minute or so, the story comes. I have been privileged to hear of the stillbirth of twins. The story had not been shared with anyone in the 50 years that had gone by since that most difficult day. Another shared the shame and pain-filled isolation of a hidden pregnancy that had ended in miscarriage. No one else had ever known. Others have expressed guilt, feeling that it was somehow wrong to carry pain, judging their grief to be less valid because their loss happened earlier in pregnancy than the losses that others had experienced.

In each of those conversations, the very act of bringing the experience into the light brought some measure of healing. It was visible in their faces. Something of the burden had been lifted. The impact of each sharing has been profound.

In every act of honest, open sharing, I speak from the place within me that has known God's healing love, and I can now speak of it, quietly and clearly. Whenever the moment for these conversations arises, I am reminded that this burden is carried close to the heart. The grief is real. Voices become softer; eyes often glisten with tears. Gestures of touch become especially gentle.

This is exactly what happened when I responded to a request to share my experience with a group of church women. Wise and deeply sensitive, the pastor knew that my story would help them to connect with their stories; too many were carrying deeply hidden grief.

After hearing a brief sharing of my story, the women were invited to take small tealight candles, symbols of the losses they carried. As the basket of candles moved from one to the next, I quietly blinked back my surprise, shocked at the number some women were taking.

Each woman was then invited to light her candles from a large central candle. Not a word was spoken. Each received all the time needed. In that respect-filled room, and as it felt right to each person, all were invited to share their story about the candles they had placed.

I blinked back further surprise. In greater number than the stories of their own losses, they shared the stories of their mother's miscarriages, stillbirths and early infant losses. Two generations of grief. A few stories expanded across more generations: their grandmothers and their daughters.

Until that day, most were unacknowledged grief.

It was a blessing and a privilege to bear witness as they set down heavy burdens, inviting healing and wholeness into the wounded and weary places of their lives. The stories were sometimes accompanied by the release of pain-filled emotions. There were tears. Having sensed the times and places where tears were deemed inappropriate or unwelcome, many were very practised at blinking them back.

The feelings of loss and the burden of grief can become so intrinsic to our being that we do not always know they are there. Until… the moment when we somehow *know* that this is the time, this is the place, and these are the people with whom, and through whom, we begin to receive the gift of healing and greater inner freedom.

It is an act of faith.
It is an act of courage.
It is an act of trust to be vulnerable,
to share our wounds with another.

I am grateful to those who accompanied me on my journey. They were incredibly wise, caring and compassionate people. I am still grateful for all they offered from the deep well of their gifts. My journals note the gifts, graces and lessons received along the way. They remain in mind and heart. And yet, I must acknowledge that none were perfect in their understanding of my experience or in the words they offered.

The gap between their support and guidance and my deep need is real and necessary. There had to be a space that was God's – and God's alone. I needed to connect with that unique place of emptiness that can only be filled by God. I would not have sought that place if it had been completely filled by human beings.

They saw their role clearly – they were there to help me find my way. These guides gently directed me toward the One whom I was seeking, even when I did not know it. They were wise enough to know that the journey could not be accomplished alone and wise enough to know that only I could do it.

We need one another. And we need our selves. We are the only human being with whom we live out our whole lives. We had best not abandon our selves.

In denying our grief and hiding our sorrow, we leave part of our selves by the side of the road. We return, in spirit, inviting healing into that time and place. We must do so in a particular way: we go back with someone.

One wise guide knew that her role, necessary as it was, also had its limitations. She knew when to step back, allowing God's healing power to come into that time and place. The wisdom of her solid admonition is deeply treasured: "Do not go back alone. Go with God. Take whomever else you want with you. Just do not go alone."

I was advised to invite the prayerful presence of particular people. Some were still alive. Some are members of the Communion of Saints. Some are recognized as official saints within the Church; many are known only to those with whom I share life. I recalled receiving a small wooden icon featuring St. Gerard Majella, patron of expectant mothers. It was the first gift I received from my mother when she learned we were expecting a baby.

It was she who kept watch over me in the hours after the miscarriage, making sure I did not hemorrhage. Although she carried deep, hidden pain from her own losses, her gifts of faith and attentive love are still held in mind and heart. She was the first person I invited to accompany me on the journey back to that time and place.

Having gone home to God, our special people are now blessed with a wisdom and a sense of peace that was not fully theirs while they lived on earth. They have graduated from the school of life and are now able to be the people they would have wanted to be while they were here, living and learning alongside us. Their love is never-ending.

Healing from the loss of our little one brings me a deeper appreciation for the enduring promise: in death, *life is changed, not ended.*

*

The story offered in these words is part of the good news – the gospel of my life. Imperfect as they are, I still trust that in them you will find gifts, graces and lessons to bless your journey.

I hope your story becomes part of the gospel of your life – the good news of the times and places in which you experienced the loving and healing compassion of Jesus, the Christ. He came to show us the way. The profoundly good news is that his love is never-ending.

***Brenda Merk Hildebrand** has a deep passion for lifelong learning, education, and spiritual and palliative care. She believes that when we die, we are simply born into eternal life.*

Remembering Mercy

Josephine Lombardi

I am a mother who has lost a child through miscarriage, the loss of a child that occurs before 20 weeks of pregnancy. Like so many parents who look forward to welcoming a new child into their lives, my husband and I were excited about this pregnancy. At the time of this loss, I was already the mother of three children. Sadly, my experience corresponds to recent statistics that one in four pregnancies ends in miscarriage.[1] My miscarriage at 15 weeks occurred during a very difficult time in my life; my mother had died only five days before. (Most miscarriages, about 75 percent, "occur within the first twelve weeks of pregnancy."[2]) We were hit with a double loss in a very short period, leaving us speechless as we tried to process all the sorrow and confusion.

Before this happened, the gift of this and all my pregnancies reminded me of the great joy of being entrusted with the precious life of a child to nurture and to raise. We were ecstatic to hear that

1 See Laura Kelly Fanucci and Franco David Fanucci, *Grieving Together: A Couple's Journey through Miscarriage* (Huntington, IN: Our Sunday Visitor, 2018), chapter 1.

2 Ibid.

my due date was March 19, 2003, as March 19 is the Solemnity of St. Joseph, the Spouse of Mary. As I have a great devotion to St. Joseph, the news of the due date brought a smile to my face. Sadly, however, for reasons unknown to us – like all other parents who have lost a child through miscarriage – this little life did not continue to grow. We lost our precious child on September 15, 2002, the Feast of Our Lady of Sorrows. Perhaps the date of the loss was a reminder that Our Lady walked before us and knows the ache of grief and loss, especially the loss of a child in horrific circumstances. Miscarriage is a painful experience because a life is lost and, along with it, all the hopes associated with the excitement of pregnancy and parenting.

I held the lifeless little body of my precious child after she was expelled from my body. I could see and touch a little body that was already formed. Prior to the release of my child's body, I had been feeling unwell for several hours, resulting in a hospital stay to stop the hemorrhage. Feeling weak and exhausted with grief and sorrow, I had only a few seconds to hold my precious child before the ambulance attendant took the body away for further examination. Broken-hearted, we were not permitted to see her little body again. Although our baby's genitalia were still developing, it was clear she was female, and we decided to name our child Mercy.[3] Naming a child is a key way of recognizing the dignity of a child, reminding parents that the child was known by God: "Before I formed you in the womb I knew you, and before you were born I consecrated you; I appointed you a prophet to the nations" (Jeremiah 1:5). Moreover, we honoured her dignity and existence by asking our priest to celebrate a Mass in her memory.

3 According to Dr. Louann Brizendine, male genitalia start to develop around eight weeks and would have been evident by 15 weeks. See Louann Brizendine, *The Female Brain* (New York: Morgan Road Books, 2006).

The *Catechism of the Catholic Church* reminds us that unborn and unbaptized infants are entrusted to "the great mercy of God," giving us hope regarding their eternal lives with God (CCC 1261). Parents who have experienced miscarriage or infant loss are reminded that they are not alone in their sorrow; resources and trained pastoral care ministers are available to assist them. "Blessing of Parents after a Miscarriage or Stillbirth,"[4] for example, is a resource prepared by the United States Conference of Catholic Bishops to assist parents in their time of grief and to "console them with the blessing of God."[5] This book offers adaptable rituals to use as well. These types of resources bring hope and encouragement, especially when there is so much confusion and heartache over the cause of the loss.

During the follow-up visit with my doctor after my miscarriage, he addressed my grief, affirming and acknowledging my sorrow and sense of confusion. Knowing I was overanalyzing the possible causes for the miscarriage, he consoled me by saying the loss was not due to something I did or did not do. The miscarriage was most likely due to internal issues, beyond my control, that prevented my child from completing her development. My loss, and the loss of so many unborn children, is most often due to "chromosomal abnormalities ... due to a problem that occurred during an early stage of the baby's development."[6] Other possible causes include "hormonal issues, infections, maternal issues" or the "fertilized egg does not implant properly into the lining of the uterus."[7]

4 See https://www.usccb.org/prayers/blessing-parents-after-miscarriage-or-stillbirth.

5 Ibid. The Order of Christian Funerals includes "Funeral Rites for Children," including special prayers for children who die without Baptism. See also the Revised Code of Canon Law 1183.2 and https://www.catholicmiscarriagesupport.com.

6 Fanucci and Fanucci, *Grieving Together*, chapter 1.

7 Ibid.

Despite the empathic and informative response delivered by my doctor, as I tried with great difficulty to find meaning in the loss, I fell into the trap of so many bereaved parents: self-blame. I had been caring for my dying mother for the duration of the pregnancy. Although I had taken some time off from work, I was working on my doctorate and had three children; the third was only one year old. I was still nursing my youngest child and I was very sleep deprived, caring for my family and my mother when she lived with us before her final two months in a palliative care unit of a local hospital. Once she was admitted, I was back and forth to the hospital several times a day, bringing food and taking care of her personal needs.

I brought my youngest back and forth with me, carrying his stroller, loading and unloading him and the stroller from my car. After the miscarriage, I kept saying to myself, "I was doing too much" or "I overexerted myself." When I shared my thoughts with my doctor, he was quick to reassure me that my child ceased to develop, and the loss was not due to overexertion. Sadly, however, it appeared that I was not the only one searching for answers. Some family members told me that my grief over the loss of my mother caused the miscarriage. Others, trying to be helpful, said, "At least you have three children" or "You will have another one." The birth of another child does not erase the memory of the lost child, nor does the new baby replace the miscarried baby. Still others, trying to offer some words of consolation, said, "It's the stress of raising three children. Stress caused the miscarriage."

These comments are what I call "level 1" responses. One of the courses I teach at St. Augustine's Seminary, where I serve as Assistant Dean for Academic Affairs and Associate Professor, is Pastoral Counselling. One of the units of this course is titled "Attentive and Empathic Listening." Throughout the unit, I walk my students through a three-level response system when it comes to responding to someone in grief or crisis.

Level 1	The response is insensitive and impulsive, paying no attention to feelings or someone's perspective. These individuals listen to respond. Examples include responses that begin with "At least..."	"At least you have three children." "At least you can get pregnant." "Be thankful you have other children." "It's God's will."[8]
Level 2	After the person listens, the response restates content and acknowledges feelings. We listen to understand feelings.	"I'm sorry for your loss. You're grieving the loss of your child/pregnancy." "You're feeling lost and overwhelmed."
Level 3	Level 2 plus perspective taking. (A more empathic response.) Empathy involves recognizing emotion, acknowledging feelings and perspective taking. Empathy communicates connection.	"I'm sorry for this loss. You were so very excited about this pregnancy. I'm here for you in this time of grief."

Responding to a bereaved person with an empathic response shows them you have taken the time to consider their

8 This response can create great discomfort and pain, confusing the bereaved regarding their image of God. Although we do not know why these losses and other tragedies are allowed or permitted, we do not help the bereaved by implying that God desired this loss. We want to encourage their faith life, not discourage it.

experience, you have acknowledged and recognized what they are feeling, and you are ready to accompany them during this difficult season. Anyone who has experienced the loss of a loved one knows we do not get *over* the loss, we get *through* it, with all the intensity and frequency of the waves of grief, by the grace of God and with the prayers and support of loved ones.

The mystery of Christ's resurrection inspired St. Paul to address the pain of grief when he wrote, "But we do not want you to be uninformed, brothers and sisters, about those who have died, so that you may not grieve as others do who have no hope" (1 Thessalonians 4:13). Hope, the habit of waiting with patience and perseverance, turns our focus away from the "why" and toward the "what," as in "What can I do now?" – not "What if?" "What if" is not helpful because it traps us in the past, knowing there is nothing we can do to change what has happened. "What can I do now?" or "What can I expect going forward?" prepares us to surrender and manage our grief.

Dr. Bill Webster, a well-known grief expert, has authored several books on the grief journey.[9] In *Now What?* he documents some emotional and physiological responses to grief:[10]

* numbness
* crying
* confusion
* physical distress, including a variety of physical symptoms (such as stomach issues, sleep issues, changes in appetite, fatigue)
* anger[11]

9 See https://griefjourney.com.

10 Bill Webster, "Now What?" (www.griefjourney.com).

11 St. Paul, in his Letter to the Ephesians (4:26), exclaimed, "Be angry but do not sin." The expression of righteous anger is part of the healing process.

* guilt
* grief attacks (waves of grief/feelings of being overwhelmed or overcome with sadness and loss)

Raising awareness about the emotional and physiological responses to grief helps the bereaved to process what they are experiencing, making them more self-aware when it comes to the experience of loss. The following is a compilation of exercises, shared by other experts,[12] recommended for the bereaved parent or the person/pastor accompanying a parent:

1. Allow yourself to grieve, remaining mindful of how the emotional response to your grief may be felt in your body. In the beginning, the waves of grief may be experienced as more frequent and intense. Sadly, the sight of other babies, baby sounds or pregnant women, for example, may trigger a new wave.
2. Share feelings with your spouse, recognizing that their grief may be expressed differently. Authors Gamino and Cooney, commenting on the needs of fathers, write, "Fathers sometimes feel forgotten when miscarriage or stillbirth happens."[13] A father's grief, they say, may be best expressed by doing something because "doing something constructive helps counteract the terrible feelings of helplessness."[14] Remembering the grief of the father and allowing the father to express grief shows we acknowledge his pain in this very difficult time. If you have other children, be mindful of their emotional response to the loss. Children may need help to process what they have experienced.

12 Some of these steps are found in Louis A. Gamino and Ann Taylor Cooney, *When Your Baby Dies through Miscarriage or Stillbirth* (Minneapolis: Augsburg Press, 2002).

13 Ibid., 30.

14 Ibid., 32.

3. If you are ready and comfortable, share your story with a trusted friend, pastor or pastoral counsellor.
4. Strive to avoid the "why," as it is difficult to find any meaning or reason for the loss, especially when the temptation to self-blame is so strong. Reject this temptation.
5. Focus on the "what" of grief, as in what can be done to manage the waves of grief. Some steps include the following:
   * Name the baby.
   * Plan a memorial for the baby or identify a keepsake to honour the child's memory.
   * Write a letter to the child, including your feelings of loss and love for them.
   * If you have a hard time praying, ask your pastor, family and friends to pray for you.
   * Talk to your pastor about options for a blessing, prayer service or memorial Mass for your child.
   * Call the chancery office of your diocese or a local Catholic agency to see if there are any bereavement supports for parents grieving the loss of a child through miscarriage or stillbirth.

During our time of loss, we were blessed with the support of our pastor and the love and encouragement of friends and family, even when they did not know how to respond. Although we experienced and shared our grief differently, we cried when the waves of grief overcame us, and we remembered our beloved Mercy with a keepsake, prayers and Masses.

We were blessed with another child, born on May 1, 2004, the Feast of St. Joseph the Worker. Our youngest daughter did not replace the child we lost, but the date of her birth is a reminder of the mercy of God. Sadly, however, I am aware that this may not be the experience of other parents who have lost a child. Sometimes pregnancy does not occur again, or there is another loss. For those with these experiences, St. Paul could be considered their patron saint. In his Second Letter to the Corinthians (12:1-10), he describes a mystical experience and the pain of a "thorn in the flesh." He prays to be delivered from this pain. Instead, our Lord responds that his grace will strengthen St. Paul, ensuring that he will not be overcome by the thorn (12:9). Unlike St. Elizabeth, whose infertility was overcome (Luke 1:36), St. Paul's thorn remained. Nevertheless, God strengthened St. Paul in his time of trial, reminding him he could manage the struggle with the help of God's grace. This applies to couples dealing with infertility as well. They, too, are called to be fruitful with their gifts and time. St. John Paul II, aware of the pain of infertility, did not limit fruitfulness to biological parents:

> To couples who cannot have children of their own I say: you are no less loved by God; your love for each other is *complete and fruitful* when it is open to others, to the needs of the apostolate, to the needs of the poor, to the needs of orphans, to the needs of the world. Infertility in a marriage is indeed a share in the suffering of Christ; but it can be, and is intended to be, one that bears fruit in the Kingdom of God.[15]

Although the pain of loss remains, and questions surrounding the loss resurface with waves of grief, our faith reminds us that God's grace strengthens us in times of loss and crisis because we are not alone. We trust that we are known and heard, and our children who died before or soon after birth are known and loved, too.

15 Pope John Paul II, Address to Families in Nigeria, February 18, 1982. (Emphasis mine.)

For it was you who formed my inward parts;
you knit me together in my mother's womb.
I praise you, for I am fearfully and wonderfully made…
My frame was not hidden from you,
when I was being made in secret,
intricately woven in the depths of the earth.
Your eyes beheld my unformed substance.
In your book were written
all the days that were formed for me,
when none of them as yet existed.

(Psalm 139:13-14a; 15-16)

***Josephine Lombardi, Ph.D.**, is the Assistant Dean for Academic Affairs and Associate Professor of Systematic and Pastoral Theology at St. Augustine's Seminary in Scarborough. She is a wife and mother of four adult children with two grandchildren, and is a published author and a frequent speaker at conferences and retreats. Visit her website at www.josephinelombardi.com.*

All the Love Needed

Ryan and Monique LeBlanc

Monique

I knew something was wrong the moment the ultrasound tech said she would be right back. I was at my 20-week structural ultrasound for my fifth child. I had done this before and knew the routine. An ultrasound tech walking out so soon – before even showing me a picture of the baby – was definitely out of the normal routine.

So, I sat waiting, alone, knowing that in a few minutes when she returned, my life would be forever changed. I just did not know how. As my thoughts raced to all the imagined possibilities, I did the one thing I knew would help. I prayed.

Prayer was and still is a big part of my life. At different times in my life, the Rosary, the Daily Office and other set prayers have been a comfort and routine, but in that moment it was none of those that came to me. It was just a desperate plea to God, almost wordless. I just knew God was there, and I needed him. I knew that in the next few minutes, God was going to give me a gift, and I was pretty sure I did not want it. I had an image of Christmas morning, with all these presents under the tree. I am sitting there with a present from my old but loving aunt. I don't know what is in it, but I know that it is not the toy I really want. It is probably ugly socks or a book I would rather not read. But I have a choice to make. When I open the gift, do I say thank you, even though it is hard to be grateful for a gift that I can't see why I would want, or do I complain and sulk because I did not get what I want? I knew that at that moment, waiting for the radiologist to come and tell me that my son had died in my womb, I had a choice to make. Was I going to accept this gift that God was giving me, a gift I did not want, knowing that in his infinite mercy, it was a gift? Or was I going to complain and sulk to God?

So, I prayed: God, help me accept this gift, this ugly gift that I do not want, because I know that it is a gift of love. I don't understand why I got this gift, and I may never know why this gift was for me, but help me accept it with grace.

Ryan

Wrangling my four young children in a mall bookstore, I felt a wave of relief when my cell phone rang. *Excellent – Monique's ultrasound is done.* My expectation hit a wall.

"It's not very good news."

On the way back to the radiologist, I experienced for the first time a pattern that would surface again and again as we journeyed through the miscarriage. When I had a very specific task to accomplish for someone else, such as explaining to my children ages two to nine that baby "Quinto" had died, and Mommy might be very sad when we picked her up, I found simple, easy strength in my spirit. The words and the tone just flowed from me without my knowing where they came from. It was the waiting, the empty space in between things to do, that made me feel completely undone, a sense of dangling over a void. Abysmal.

At home, the kids went and played. We made some phone calls to our family. But then there was just emptiness: questions I didn't want to think of and couldn't imagine what an answer would look like. An incapacity to think, plan, understand. An overwhelming feeling that I couldn't feel, which pushed out everything else, but was completely hidden to me.

While we would appreciate every medical professional who worked with us throughout the experience, we had very little information about what the process involved. For all our other children, we were accustomed to a high level of informed consent, thoughtful discussion with our caregivers, a shared journey of health and spiritual meaning.

Now we had an appointment tomorrow with the hospital's admissions office, and that was all. Nothing else but empty space until morning, in our room, in our hearts. Holy Saturday, but inside us.

At the hospital, there was very little procedure to be done: we started to induce labour, and then we waited. Monique and I had so much time, and the emptiness began to take shape in our attempts to form words. We talked it through: the disbelief, the numbness, the surreal character of our situation, forgetting for a moment where we were and why. We talked around in circles, we talked back and forth on the same point, we avoided the topic, we spoke the obvious out loud. How much can you analyze the ladies' pink hunting rifle advertisements in the waiting room magazine? While it was both agonizing and boring, and we did not want to be there, as I look back it was very necessary and graced. We had to be locked up with this reality, this loss, for this seemingly monstrous amount of time. We had to see each other in this moment as we really were if we were to come to some kind of understanding of ourselves. A conclave to name our grief.

We prayed. Nothing really coherent or organized. Avoiding prayer was as much a prayer as speaking. The grace we were given was the grace to remember God's infinite goodness and the grace to tell him how this dumpster-fire shitstorm had absolutely nothing to do with goodness.

Monique cried. It would come, it would go. We would laugh, we would pause, we would start to think and then quickly do something else. Inducing labour took us through the whole day into the night, and eventually contractions showed up to give us something to focus on. That deep darkness of the middle of the night, the tired and wrought feelings, the engulfing pangs which were familiar yet wrong. Again, being strong and present for my wife doing the hardest thing she'll ever do gave me focus and purpose. And after it was over, when I held my son, the abyss held me, and I cried hard.

We were so raw. We slept at the hospital before returning home. The one thing we had to do was done – now what? God was still present to us, sitting in the ashes of our devastation with us. But he also showed up in the family and friends who supported us. My cousin spent the night with our children while we were in the hospital. My father brought food. The first friend we made in the city, just a week earlier, came by to listen and care. Our new parish's newly ordained priest clicked on "Miscarriage Resources" on the diocesan website and had everything he needed organized for him so he could be emotionally present in his ministry to us. Monique's sister and mother flew in for the service.

We were so well cared for, as much as could be, and as much as every grieving parent deserves. It did not lift the spiritual and emotional weight, but it kept that weight clean without adding to it. This was how I experienced God's presence and help through the loss. He was there and he kept me safe from the poison that I might have turned to in my heart. Poisons of avoidance, substance, bitterness, despair, withdrawal, violence. Driven by my hurt, those could have driven my hurt deeper down and twisted it such that the healing would be impeded.

Monique

The memorial Liturgy of the Word for my son, Hilary Julian, was gut-wrenchingly beautiful. Until the week of my miscarriage, I didn't even know there was a memorial rite for an unbaptized baby. Because of the work of healing and grieving that I had been busy with, Ryan had taken care of all the arrangements. To be honest, I did not know what to expect. Not only that: because we had just moved halfway across the country less than a month before, I had no idea if there would be anyone there. But I had forgotten that as a Catholic, I am part of a huge family. A new friend that we had just met a week before came and sang along with Ryan's cousin. People came from far and wide, including my mother and sister, who flew in from Victoria. Surrounded by these people, I felt loved and supported. This feeling of love continued to grow as the familiar words of the Church were spoken: "In the name of the Father, and of the Son, and of the Holy Spirit." Yes, I was here in grief, sadness and confusion, but I was also here in the Father, the Son and the Holy Spirit. I was not alone in my grief; I was surrounded by love.

Part of the service was a litany of the saints. As the beautiful music of the litany filled the space, I realized that this small chapel was also filled with these saints, invisibly occupying the pews left empty. Yes, many of the pews were filled with family and friends, but they would need to go home later in the day. But I would never be left alone in my grief. I had a whole heavenly family who would be with me every step of this journey. I could call on them at 2 a.m. when everyone else was asleep. I could call on them when Ryan's own grief made it hard for him to carry mine. I was here in the arms of God and his people, holding me up when I felt unable to hold myself up. I did not need to have it all together, because the people around me, the angels, the saints and God himself were there to hold me together while I fell apart.

Ryan

The moment of liturgy and interment was natural and familiar to me. It was something that I did not need to find the strength to do; instead, it gave me focus and purpose. I could be fully who I was in that moment, and those who loved me could gather around me and strengthen me by their presence. I could be both silent and expressive with the words that formed my prayer for me.

I wrote that my son's beauty was hidden, because his little body was tough to look at. I wished I could have had an earthly life with him, to see him grow and hear his voice. I knew that for his whole life, he knew nothing but the love of his mother surrounding him, and now he knows the love of his heavenly Father surrounding him.

For the rest of my life, in addition to having a heavenly Father, I have a heavenly son, who is closer to me in some ways than my earthly children. In my deepest needs, I still turn to him to pray for me and our family. And one day, he will welcome me home.

Monique

All my life I have had a deep sense of the goodness of our Creator and the love of God. Even in my questioning adolescence and my 20s, while I found my own relationship with the Church, I knew in my bones that I was loved and cared for by God. But after the loss of my baby, my spirituality changed, grew and deepened. There were days that I was so angry with God for taking my son that it was hard to see the goodness around me. The weeks and months after my loss were full of bright blue skies, trips to the pool and evenings of fireworks. With a busy house with four children, I had to keep moving and living, but it felt like I was only half there. I knew God was still good, because I could see it in the colour of the early fall trees, hear it in my children's laughter and feel it in the warmth of the sun. But how could it all be true when my baby had been born into the palm of my hand, silent, limp and small? Then came a storm of icy winds and blowing snow that hit my window with a sound that matched my heart. The world looked as angry and sad as I felt. The words of the canticle from the Book of Daniel ran through my mind;

> All you winds, bless the Lord.
> Fire and heat, bless the Lord,
> Cold and chill, bless the Lord.
> Dew and rain, bless the Lord.
> Frost and chill, bless the Lord.
> Ice and snow, bless the Lord.

My God is not only the Lord of the good times, the Lord of the comfortable. He is the Lord of the wind and the Lord of the ice. He loves me in and through the anger and hurt and confusion of this loss. He can take my shattered heart and hold it while I cry and rage like the early winter storm. And then, if I let him in, he can slowly and beautifully rebuild it, stronger than it was before. Even now, years later, I come back to that canticle when life feels overwhelming. Now, in the face of pain, anger and despair, I know in my core that I have a God who can and will stand by me in this moment, no matter how hard it is.

Hilary Julian LeBlanc

August 23, 2013

The Eternal Father, out of his tender care,
has willed to share with us, along with the grace to bear it,
a portion of the Divine Love with which he looked down
on his broken Son at Calvary.

The grief of Eve, of Jacob, of David,
and of our Blessed Mother
has become our grief, and our grace,
surrounding us with the solidarity of those parents
who lost their children,
who hold us in their understanding and sympathy.

We gave Hilary all the love he needed here on Earth.
Yet we had more – much more – to give.
The pain in our hearts is that enormous love
that our son suddenly outgrew,
as he went on into his Heavenly Father's arms,
where all his needs are met,
and the love he receives is infinite.

Now that we have successfully led him to Heaven,
the Father wills for us
to pour out our love for Hilary
into the world, toward the tiny and helpless ones,
loving with the same trust and surrender that Hilary lived.

To help us in this, we have a Heavenly Father,
and now we have a heavenly son,
who does not receive our care, but,
through his prayers before the throne of God,
cares for us,
to strengthen our family in the Communion of Saints.

We open our hands, we raise them to Heaven,
and we release our pride and our control.
The life we would have willed for Hilary,
the life we would have bound our hearts and souls to,
is not so holy and perfect as the life God gave him
nor, in Eternity, so long.

In the glory of the Resurrection
we will feel Hilary wrap his arms around us,
in fulfilment of this present moment's embrace,
his love which we cannot see or touch,
but will go with us from here
until our tiny saint welcomes us into our Big Life.

***Ryan** and **Monique LeBlanc** have been married more than 20 years; they make their home in Saskatoon, which is in Treaty Six Territory and the traditional homeland of the Métis. They have five children with them on Earth and one – Hilary – in heaven. Monique homeschools their three youngest children and previously contributed to the anthology* Love Rebel: Reclaiming Motherhood. *Ryan serves the Catholic school system as a Teacher Chaplain and is in formation toward ordination to the Permanent Diaconate with the Diocese of Saskatoon.*

Bittersweet and Imperfect Joy

Leah Perrault

I never asked, "Why me?" Since one in four pregnancies ends with loss, I began preparing for the possibility with our first. Marc shushed me after one of our prenatal classes when I wondered (a little too) aloud why they weren't telling us what would happen if our baby died. I needed to know if I would be able to hold the tiny one on the outside. Even after we delighted in the first cries of three healthy babies, I reminded myself often that they aren't mine, but God's. I have not been promised a life that ends before theirs.

We were living in Toronto, far from our family in Saskatchewan, when we found out we were pregnant with our Robyn. Marc was moving home several months ahead of me, and so we made the decision to tell our family and friends at just six weeks pregnant. Though there was some skepticism about our early news, most were delighted to celebrate with us. It was a tradition we kept for all four of the next pregnancies. I wanted to delight in new life with our loved ones – even if it meant that we would someday have to share the news of a loss.

Over the years our family was growing, I was working as the Director of Pastoral Services in the Diocese of Saskatoon. There was a beautiful miscarriage support ministry growing in those years, and at work and in my personal life, I had the heartbreak and privilege of walking with people who experienced both miscarriage and infant loss. I learned so much about how these beautiful and longed-for babies and their families could be grieved and carried and loved.

In January of 2017, we were ecstatic to learn that we were pregnant with our fourth baby. Robyn, Eliot and Charlize were eager to make space for her; we moved a bedroom because the kids were so excited. We were planning a summer holiday with friends, and the dates and location were chosen in light of how pregnant I would be. With each of my five children, I have marvelled at the way our whole world changes as soon as we know they exist.

February 9, I was driving home from working in a neighbouring city and felt the first twinges – way too much like labour for my liking. When I called my midwife to talk about the bleeding, she said, "It could go either way. Rest. And pray." Before the sun rose the next morning, I delivered a tiny baby, 10 weeks along, into the palm of my hand. She was perfect in every way, except that she was lying deathly still in my hands, 30 weeks too early.

I could count all 10 fingers and toes. The chambers of her heart were outlined against her chest. She already had the signature curved nose all our babies shared. I carried her into the bedroom and lay on the bed with Marc, crying for the life we had hoped for her. We named her Claire. In the earliest hours of the morning, long before the February sun rose and our bigger kids woke from sleep, we loved her for the only minutes we would get with her body on earth.

Maybe because we had stumbled innocently onto sharing pregnancy news early, or because of all the babies I had cried for with their heartbroken parents, or because of my work in ministry, I knew that we could choose the way we grieved and honoured Claire. I knew that some people would not understand or would try to dismiss our grief because she was so very young and losses are too common. But I was not interested in participating in the tradition of minimizing miscarriage.

That first morning, I called in to say I wasn't going to be at work, and I quietly made pancakes for the big kids. Rather than the usual bus and commuting routines, we drove them where they needed to go. I pulled up at daycare to the most stunning Saskatoon sunrise, purple and pink and orange. It still surprises me that the world can be so beautiful when my heart is so broken.

While the kids carried out a usual day, we phoned our parents and siblings one at a time to share our sad news. They cried with us, and I was never more grateful that this was not their introduction to Claire. It was so profoundly helpful that I had memories of their joy for her as well as their sorrow.

Knowing that we would have to tell the kids, I took a nap and then got up to make sugar cookies – a favourite activity of mine and theirs. And when they arrived home, we decorated them together as Marc and I told them that their tiniest sister had died in my tummy. They wanted to know where she was, so we took her out of the fridge where we had placed her in a medicine cup, and they marveled at the miracle of this tiny person revealed on the outside.

The next day, we delivered those cookies to other families who had lost babies, and my oldest girl carried my youngest girl into the funeral home. Many funeral homes will cremate miscarried babies at no charge. They returned us to her in the tiniest little urn. I called my grandma and asked if we could bury Claire with my grandpa. The conversation turned into the most amazing gift. Grandma had lost a baby just before my dad, and none of us had known about it. Sharing about our loss allowed her to share about hers. And if Grandma hadn't lost that baby, my dad wouldn't have been born.

We planned a Mass at our parish in a small chapel and invited our family and friends. Not everyone came, and that was okay. The ones who needed to be there showed up and grieved with us for Claire and for their own losses. One of my aunts had lost several grandchildren, and as she hugged me after, she whispered her thanks: "I needed this for mine, too."

I took time off work. I felt guilty about it at the time, but the recovery from the miscarriage was so much more physically difficult than the full-term births. It was like my body did not know how to be so suddenly robbed of life. And my workplace was invited to honour both my recovery and my grief as sick time. (Thankfully, they were very generous and kind – which they might not have been – but if I hadn't told them, I would never have known.) In those weeks following, I slept, received gifts of meals made for my family and let other people clean my house. It was so affirming to have others recognize the depth of the loss and my need for care, along with Marc and the kids.

My kids were so sad, and I wondered if we had done the right thing in telling them so soon. We might have spared them such aching grief. But they also made such beautiful connections to living and dying, in nature and their observations of relationships and eventualities. In sharing with them, we also gave them the chance to celebrate and grieve a sister. And their innocent grieving and living was such a gift for me in my own.

About a month later, I wrote about it in my monthly column, sharing publicly. More people reached out to share their own stories of loss and express their care and support for us. And many expressed how our willingness to talk about Claire gave them permission to talk about and grieve their own losses, some of them decades past.

Maybe the hardest part for me about the miscarriage was that my body felt like a tomb. This part of me that was supposed to deliver new life teeming into the world had become the scene of a death. I needed to leave the place of the death, and I couldn't because I *was* the place. And so, I sought out intentionally the experiences of joy and life and laughter that reminded me that my body was still very much alive. Singing at the top of my lungs with other people. Letting myself laugh until I cried. Tenderly asking Marc to make love, even if I cried.

In the months that followed Claire's death, I stopped hearing God. I scarcely had words to pray. But I was bathed with colour in the silence. I would close my eyes and open them again, and it was like I was wearing coloured glasses. The world bathed in purple and a deep sense of comfort and peace. Washed over in red and the sensation of being carried. Swirling blue and green and feeling lost in a mystery. The silence was deafening, and I cannot imagine how much harder it would have been to navigate without telling everyone.

Here's the thing. I've always been so skeptical of the ways that our culture and sometimes even our church communities downplay miscarriage. There are so many hurtful things that get said:

"It wasn't meant to be."

"God loved this one too much for life on earth."

"You'll try again and have another."

"It was so early; just get over it."

The sting was quick because I knew the words weren't for me. Each of us is an unrepeatable miracle that is not promised anything other than our existence in each present moment. Claire changed our world just by growing in the dark and secret for 10 weeks. She expanded my heart, brought joy to our family, rearranged our plans. Her heart beat alongside mine, and her cells multiplied within me.

By sharing her with others, we dared to proclaim that her life mattered to us.

And then, we dared to proclaim that her death mattered, too.

We learned to say new things:

"I'm so sorry your baby died. It hurts so much, and we are here for you."

"Did you name your baby? I would love to pray by name."

"God grieves with you."

"There is no timeline for grief. The only way out is through, at your own pace."

The spring slowly emerged from our grief, and the days got longer and the ground thawed as the snow melted. Easter came, and we began to plan a time when we would be able to bury her beside my grandpa. But before we could, my twin sister Abbie was murdered. Our hearts broke all over again, and we discovered that Claire was still giving us gifts.

She gave us intimate, first-hand experience with a death by natural (rather than violent) causes in our immediate family. She showed us that grief could be lived through. She showed us with butterflies and colour and dreams that she was not gone but with us. God did not cause Claire's death but would not waste it. We believe that death is never the final word; the Creator of everything always turns death into new life.

We buried Claire in her tiny urn with Abbie, right beside my grandpa. A friend received the gift of a dream with Abbie holding Claire and some other special babes in her arms. There is living and dying, and there is rising, and the way that we grieve honours all of it. Just a week after we buried them both, we found out we were expecting Atticus. A new baby who wouldn't have existed if we hadn't lost Claire. A bittersweet and imperfect joy.

May we honour the tiniest ones who give us hope and a changed world.

May we grieve and remember them and all they teach us.

May we anticipate our reunion with them in eternity.

Amen.

Leah Perrault *is an author and speaker in Swift Current, Saskatchewan, on Treaty 4 Territory. She works as Executive Director of Southwest Homes. You can follow her work at www.leahperrault.com.*

Reflections from a Doctor and Mother

Julia Cataudella, MD

In the early days of my marriage in 2005, I began to ask God to *increase my love*. At that point, I was already a medical doctor, in independent practice for two years. I had experienced an intense ignition and profound deepening of my Catholic faith during my medical school years through activi ties at the University Catholic Chaplaincy and had been set on fire with the teachings of the Church on marriage and sexuality in documents such as *Humanae vitae, Love and Responsibility* and *Theology of the Body.* I had responded to Pope St. Paul VI's "call to men of science" to help women and couples learn about the signs of their fertility and to advance humanity in the application of this knowledge, and its deeper meaning, toward the "spacing of births."[16]

It followed that this would lead to the empowerment of women and spouses in their marital love, and it also would become a powerful tool in the hands of doctors aiming to evaluate

16 *Humanae vitae*, 24.

and manage reproductive health issues in a way that cooperates with, heals and supports the natural system that God created. Family Medicine Residency became my path to providing the much-needed fertility awareness–based methods to women and couples. During my residency, I completed training at the Pope Paul VI Institute for the Study of Human Reproduction in Omaha, Nebraska. The result was a double certificate as a Natural Family Planning Medical Consultant, applying principles of NaPro (Natural Procreative) Technology,[17] and as a Creighton Model *FertilityCare* Practitioner (instructor).[18] My first independent year led me to focus my practice in NaPro. I became very active as a speaker on marital love to youth groups, women's groups, medical bioethics symposia, many Catholic marriage preparation programs, and even foreign missions. I began applying my specialized knowledge in helping couples struggling with infertility or miscarriages, or any other ailment of the reproductive system, through this cooperative approach.

Nonetheless, I knew that my love was not as it could be. God's answer soon arrived clearly with the conception of our first child. The now St. John Paul II had recently told the youth of the world that, with the help of our love of Jesus in the Eucharist, it is possible to forget ourselves and be open to the joy of self-giving love. The Eucharist helps us to transition from a love of feelings to a love of actions: "For love is not merely a feeling; it is an act of will that consists of preferring, in a constant manner, the good of others to the good of oneself: 'Greater love has no man than this, that a man lays down his life for his friends' (Jn 15:13)."[19]

17 https://naprotechnology.com, updated © 2023.

18 https://creightonmodel.com, updated Copyright © 2023 Creighton Model.

19 Message of the Holy Father John Paul II to the Youth of the World on the Occasion of the XIX World Youth Day 2004, "We want to see Jesus" (Jn 12:21).

I knew from my own hormonal history and knowledge of my underlying reproductive health issues that this baby was at risk, so I said to him quietly, in the earliest days, "Hang in there, baby!" With much-needed hormonal support, but not without my experiencing metabolic disturbance with severe weight gain of pregnancy, Daniel made it. So did Anthony, 17 months later, minus the metabolic disturbance, on Pentecost Sunday, Mother's Day, 33 days after the death of my mother, just after the Feast of Divine Mercy! These details have meaning, as do all things when we are trusting that God knows all, sees all, feels all and lets nothing pass without his loving and merciful approval. These consoling details would help me to mourn the loss of my mom, while being busy with two babies and struggling with part-time but demanding work, in addition to my duties at home. I had attended to patients who had miscarried and was aware that in some way, I had not been able to fully understand or adequately empathize with what they were going through, until my next pregnancy…

Our third baby, Francis, was well until some spotting at 13 weeks led me to a local emergency department, where I learned that his heart was no longer beating and that his growth had stopped within the previous few days. This was my ship to the sea of compassion on the depths of reproductive loss. Naturally, we ask ourselves, "How did this happen? When and why did this happen? What was I doing when this happened?" With the dating of the baby's size, we can easily retrace our steps and imagine the answers to these questions, which is as natural as when any human death occurs in our lives so close by. The unborn baby lives in a world hidden to us, and we cannot usually learn of exactly how this loss came to be, adding inherent mystery that can make it harder to cope.

Miscarriage generally refers to the loss of a pregnancy before the baby is developed enough to survive on his or her own in any way: currently, this is 20 weeks' gestation. Fetal deaths after 20 weeks are referred to as stillbirths, and together, these are sometimes referred to as "non-live births." The pooled risk of miscarriage is considered to be around 15%,[20] or 15 to 25%,[21] of all recognized pregnancies, increasing with maternal age and number of previous miscarriages. Non-recognized pregnancies have been difficult to study, and therefore to measure, though this number may be impacted by the use of hormonal or IUD contraceptives, if we define the start of life as the moment of conception, since one of the mechanisms of these methods is failure of implantation, the rate of which varies by product and individual. Far fewer pregnancies, 2 to 3%, are lost in the second trimester, and after 20 weeks, the statistic is less than 1% (prior to 2021).[22]

As for the causes, medically, there are maternal factors and fetal factors, though mother and baby are essentially one in body until the baby and placenta are delivered. The placenta is an organ that forms between them, anchoring the baby to the mother and connecting their bodies through an intricate, expanding and developing system of blood vessels and glandular tissues. Since the maternal body is the "host" for the placental and fetal development, the state of her health and the structure of her tissues are very important and may well be modifiable, when identified and understood. There can be multiple contributing

20 S. Quenby et al., "Miscarriage Matters: The Epidemiological, Physical, Psychological, and Economic Costs of Early Pregnancy Loss," *The Lancet* 397:10285 (May 1, 2021): 1658–67.

21 Public Health Agency of Canada, "Chapter 7 Infographic: Perinatal Loss in Canada," https://www.canada.ca/en/public-health/services/publications/healthy-living/infographic-perinatal-loss-canada.html.

22 UC Davis Health website, Department of Obstetrics and Gynecology, Sacramento, CA, © 2023 UC Regents, *https://health.ucdavis.edu/obgyn/services/family-planning/trimester_loss.html.*

factors, including the health of the father. Besides the fact that his health contributes to the health of the sperm and therefore the ensuing development of the fetus after fertilization, his immune system interacts with the mother's, as can his microbiome, which may impact maternal–fetal health in various ways.

When evaluating for potential causes of miscarriage, areas to consider typically include hormonal issues, anatomy and physiology, immunology, blood flow or clotting issues, blood vessel development, such as related to hormonal or nutrient deficiencies, genetic and chromosomal, and even microbiological. Cervical insufficiency, abdominal trauma, connective tissue disorder and chronic disease are added as contributors for losses after 12 weeks, though many times the doctor will not be able to explain why the loss happened.[23]

What happens next? My steps over the days and weeks after finding that Francis had died opened my eyes to the *process* of spontaneous loss of an unborn baby. The typical questions arose, including: How and when would he come out? Would I be able to obtain his body intact for burial? There is a waiting to see the doctor and to determine the best plan, the feeling of general unwellness of a body and soul that knows their child died inside and is working to prepare for its delivery, and the having to go to work and to see people during those days when the baby is still there, but not living. This can be a horrific experience that no words can really express. Yet, I know that grace abounds and the Lord is always near. Anger and horror aside, God is present and loving each mother through this time.

I realized, as an MD, that doctors were generally not experts in the management of the remains of a "fetal demise." I needed

23 K. Danielsson, "Causes of Miscarriage in Second Trimester," Very Well Family website, updated November 29, 2022, https://www.verywellfamily.com/what-causes-second-trimester-miscarriages-2371490.

to find answers, knowing that whatever means by which this baby would come out, there was a need for me to obtain his body, even though I did not know how or what I would do next. On the occasion of Francis, the complete passage of the uterine contents did not succeed naturally. Thankfully, however, his tiny body was gently extracted, as it was found in the cervical canal by the on-call obstetrician in the Emergency department and placed on a surgical side table. Having asked my obstetrician in advance about what I could do to obtain the baby's body, he had given me a specimen bottle and invited me to save any material I would like tested (this was not exactly what I had meant). Seeing his little body on the table near me, I simply asked the nurse, with my heart racing, "Can I have that?" She said, "I'm not sure… Okay," as she walked out. Relieved, I carefully placed him in the specimen jar, puzzling over what the next step would be. Over the next two weeks, I was heartbroken; my then spiritual director found the path by which this baby would come to rest, and that process was astounding to me.

My priest spiritual director informed me that Francis' remains should be buried in consecrated ground, and that the local Catholic cemetery would accept the remains for interment on "compassionate grounds" – essentially, free of charge. I then found that he would have to be brought there by a funeral home. At the time, Catholic Cemeteries near me did not yet have their own. A local secular funeral home responded with compassion and professionalism at minimal to no cost, receiving and preparing the body, arranging it with care and beauty, offering visitation, which for me remained private, and transferring him to the cemetery plot. I was moved that the language, reverence and care that both the secular funeral home and the Catholic cemetery provided him with were no different than if Francis had been 12 years old at the time of death, which is as it should be. While the culture of our time appears to state otherwise, the human person knows at heart the full humanity of the unborn child. Our priest met my husband and me at the cemetery and recited prayers at the burial. There could be no baptism involved, and no funeral. However, as I was assured, his soul would rest in peace with the Innocents, where he could now intercede on our behalf.

All doctors practising NaProTechnology have attested and adhere to a Code of Ethics that is in keeping with the teachings of the Church on matters of human life and sexuality. The human person exists from the moment of conception, and life is sacred from conception until natural death. The empowerment of knowledge that came with decoding the signs of fertility and the consequent hormonal map created by charting those signs led to a medical understanding and approach that differs from conventional obstetrics and gynecology in the following ways:

1. Miscarriage is *always an abnormality* rather than a "normal" reproductive event. We are commonly told, "Don't worry, this is *normal* and *common*." Conventional medical practice considers miscarriage to be a relatively "normal" occurrence, until at least two or three have occurred, and then couples are referred for specialist consultation. Doctors who apply NaProTechnology approaches hold that miscarriages are *not normal* and that even the first one can potentially be prevented.[24] NaProTechnology does so by providing medical treatments and surgeries that cooperate completely with the reproductive system.[25] Babies were not meant to die in the womb any more than disease and death were meant to exist before the Fall. God came to save us from this. He provides

24 T. Hilgers, *The Medical & Surgical Practice of NaProTECHNOLOGY*, Pope Paul VI Institute Press, 2004.

25 https://naprotechnology.com, updated © 2023.

means to heal disease and to prevent untimely death, as according to his will.

2. There are *always underlying causes* of miscarriage, though we do not always know what they are, as described above. Not knowing the factors involved can make it more difficult for the couple to process and adequately grieve the loss.[26]
3. The "fetus" is a *human person*; his or her *body is sacred* and must be treated with the same respect and dignity due to any person after death (see below).
4. We acknowledge that there is a *tremendous sense of loss* that both the mother and the father may experience as a result of the death of their unborn child at any stage. Further, with recurrent miscarriages, the impact on the mother and father is intensified and can impact health very deeply: physically, mentally and spiritually. The losses are never forgotten. The sorrow is carried in the heart, mysteriously deepening the potential joy, in God's love and mercy.

Francis was to become the first of seven of our 11 children who would not live to see the light of our day. Four of the seven miscarriages would occur in the second trimester. Regarding how these losses can proceed, as a doctor and as a mother, I am aware of the range of possibilities, as they vary by gestational age and clinical context. At any stage of gestation, the baby and placenta may be delivered vaginally, and this is the ideal resolution. In the early weeks of pregnancy, it may be very difficult to obtain any remains of the baby. Where possible, tissue fragments can be kept aside for burial. After eight weeks' gestation, it is increasingly possible that the tiny baby's body can be found. Any remnants felt or known to be of the baby can be saved for burial. After 11 weeks, it is much easier to obtain the baby's body through vaginal delivery.

26 Hilgers, *The Medical & Surgical Practice of NaProTECHNOLOGY.*

There are times when vaginal delivery of the baby and placental tissue is not possible or successful. Then, a surgical dilatation and curettage (D&C) may be done by an obstetrician/gynecologist. In this case, to obtain the fetal remains, the mother or father must request that the medical staff arrange the release of the remains from the pathology department following the procedure. The staff would have the parent complete and sign a form authorizing the release of the remains from pathology, usually to a funeral home recipient, as arranged by the parent.

When surgical management is required, with the mother under general anesthesia, in the operating room, the gynecologist inserts an instrument through the vagina and into the uterus in order to remove the fetal and placental remains. In this case, I would recommend that, if possible, before the start of the surgery, the mother or father ask the gynecologist to try his or her best to pull out the baby intact. Though it may be possible, it is not very likely; this procedure results in the removal of the baby and placental material in fragments, which are sent together with fluid from surgery to the pathology department. As requested, the bag containing these contents would be released to the parents, usually as is, containing the fetal remains. This experience can be *very* devastating, since the baby did not come out in one piece. The mother may have a sentiment that a "therapeutic abortion" was done: it was not! Care of the remains from there, interred together, is a great gift to the little person, who will be met with a glorified body at the final Resurrection.

If it is not possible to inter the remains in a Catholic cemetery, the Church teaches in the Instruction *Ad Resurgendum Cum Christo* that the place of rest should be marked with the baptismal name, and the site blessed by a priest with an act of consecration using holy water. Since the unborn child does not have a baptismal name, I recommend that a name be given to the child, who was named by God in the womb (see, for example, Isaiah 49:1; Jeremiah 1:5; Galatians 1:15; Psalm 139:15-16). The processes of burial are proper to the sacredness of the human person and are helpful for closure, ongoing commemoration and eternal vision.

Through my vocation and my personal experience, I have come to sense what is a tremendous burden to mothers of recurrent miscarriage, though this suffering can be felt deeply by any woman experiencing miscarriage: the loss to the mother of the baby who has not been seen or held outside the womb; the desire to connect with the baby physically and emotionally in the ways we are used to, intensified by the knowledge that this experience was lost. I have heard women express that it felt as if their baby was ripped away from them violently, even when they experienced their miscarriage at the earliest stages of gestation.

I remember being asked during pregnancy if I wanted a boy or a girl. I would answer, "I really do not have a preference." That was always the case, even though my surviving babies were all boys. Invariably, I would be met with "Right! As long as they are healthy!" Reflecting on why this response bothered me, I realized that it was because I hadn't held or gazed at my miscarried babies before they died. I realized what a gift it would have been for me to hold my living child, even if he was born unwell or gravely ill, before he died. The gift of the child's life, and the powerful mystery of the parent–child relationship, meant so much more than could any particular feature of that little person. So, my answer became: "Not necessarily healthy, but a *living* child. One that I can hold and know, and comfort, and even say goodbye to. A *living* child."

That is something to consider when we are thinking about our *wants* with respect to children. Are children things to be wanted, or are they persons – gifts to be loved? We are called to love unconditionally; therein lies our own happiness. After recurrent losses, one of my most heartfelt devotions became that to The Seven Sorrows of Our Lady. Mary had seven sorrows, or perhaps even nine.[27] Some of these sorrows, if not all of them, were deeply united with her joys. For example, the Presentation of Our Lord and the Finding of Jesus in the Temple are both Joyful Mysteries of the Rosary as well as Sorrows of Mary. There is something mysterious connecting our sorrows in this life with our joys in this life and in the next. It is a paradox. In the Lord, the depths of my most heartfelt sorrows are somehow transformed into the heights of my greatest joys.

The other mystery I have perceived is that, in our suffering and darkness, Jesus unites with us in very profound ways. He is our greatest and most intense consolation and joy. He is our Infant, who gives himself to the mourning mother to love and to care for. Jesus receives our love, and he loves the love of us mothers toward him in his Infancy. He showed this to me one very early morning after three consecutive *completely* sleepless nights following the diagnosis of the death of our ninth baby, the sixth miscarriage: a boy of 16 weeks, only six months after the death of our previous baby boy at 16 weeks' growth. My faith had been so tested, I was relating in spirit to Job. After the third night of unrest, as my eyes closed more heavily, just after having recited a rosary in desperation at 3:00 a.m., I was met with the Presence of the Infant Jesus, brimming in splendour and inviting me, mentally, spiritually and physically, to embrace him. He knew I had needed to see that baby – *all* of those babies – and his answer was himself, given to me as a baby. So, on the third day, I awoke with my heart on fire and brimming with joy, thankful to my baby, Joseph Emanuele, for sending Jesus to me,

27 K. Hahn, "The Sorrows and Joys of Our Lady," presented at Dynamic Women of Faith Virtual Conference, May 2020.

and I chose to trust in the Lord. The Infant Jesus gives himself also to you as your Child.

Jesus Resurrected gazes into our eyes with love and sorrow, matching in his sentiments everything we have felt in the losses of our babies and in all the intricacies of our struggles in life. He knows and understands you perfectly and infinitely, parents and children, and wants to give you his infinite love, peace and joy. May we meet our beloved ones in the splendour of God's glory, united in his love, light and unsurpassable joy, for all eternity.

***Julia Cataudella, MD** is a Catholic, pro-life, women's and family medical doctor, wife and mother of four boys, with seven in heaven. Her heart is lit aflame for truth and love.*

References

Danielsson, K. "Causes of Miscarriage in Second Trimester." Very Well Family website, updated November 29, 2022, https://www.verywellfamily.com/what-causes-second-trimester-miscarriages-2371490.

Hahn, K. "The Sorrows and Joys of Our Lady." Presented at Dynamic Women of Faith Virtual Conference, May 2020.

Hilgers, T. *The Medical & Surgical Practice of NaProTECHNOLOGY* (Pope Paul VI Institute Press, 2004). See chapter 27, "Recurrent Spontaneous Abortion: Evaluation and Treatment," 775–96, and chapter 28, "Early Pregnancy Loss: Challenging Current Paradigms," 797–801.

John Paul II. *Theology of the Body*. Pauline Books & Media, 2006.

John Paul II. Message of the Holy Father John Paul II to the Youth of the World on the Occasion of the XIX World Youth Day 2004: "We want to see Jesus" (Jn 12:21).

Michels, T., Col (Ret.), MC, USA, and Alvin Y. Tiu, LTC, MC, USAAm. "Second Trimester Pregnancy Loss." *American Family Physician* 76:9 (2007), 1341–46. https://www.aafp.org/pubs/afp/issues/2007/1101/p1341.html.

Mueleman, T. et al. "HLA Associations and HLA Sharing in Recurrent Miscarriage: A Systematic Review and Meta-analysis." *Human Immunology* 76:5 (2015), 362–73.

Paul VI. Encyclical Letter *Humanae vitae*. Liberia Editrice Vaticana, 1968.

Public Health Agency of Canada. "Chapter 7 Infographic: Perinatal Loss in Canada." https://www.canada.ca/en/public-health/services/publications/healthy-living/infographic-perinatal-loss-canada.html. Date modified: 2021-04-26. For references, consult Chapter 7: "Loss and Grief in Public Health Agency of Canada." *Family-Centred Maternity and Newborn Care: National Guidelines*. Ottawa (ON): PHAC, 2020.

Quenby, S., et al. "Miscarriage Matters: The Epidemiological, Physical, Psychological, and Economic Costs of Early Pregnancy Loss." *The Lancet* 397:10285 (May 1, 2021), 1658–67. https://www.thelancet.com/journals/lancet/article/PIIS0140-6736(21)00682-6/fulltext.

Tham, Elizabeth, Karen Schliep and Joseph Stanford. "Natural Procreative Technology for Infertility and Recurrent Miscarriage: Outcomes in a Canadian Family Practice." *Canadian Family Physician* 58:5 (May 2012), e267–e274.

UC Davis Health website, Department of Obstetrics and Gynecology, Sacramento, CA, © 2023 UC Regents. https://health.ucdavis.edu/obgyn/services/family-planning/trimester_loss.html.

Wooden, C. "Final Resting Place: Vatican Releases Instruction on Burial, Cremation." *National Catholic Reporter*, October 25, 2016. https://www.ncronline.org/final-resting-place-vatican-releases-instruction-burial-cremation.

A Flurry of Stardust

How Poetry Helped Me Heal from Loss

Anna Eastland

When I lost my baby Josephine in labour, my world was shattered. I felt unsafe and off-kilter – like I had been knocked out of orbit and was spinning off into space. I prayed hard for a miracle. I prayed she would suddenly begin to live. Blood from her tiny nose ran red on my chest but she did not move. Part of me wanted to die. Part of me just had.

At that time, I did not know that the miracle I begged for would come later, and in unexpected ways. I did not know that my daughter, who never drew a breath or spoke a word through her own sweet lips, would speak powerfully to the world through me. Through my pain expressed and shared in poetry, Josephine would help bring solace to others who suffer.

Josephine

Josephine flashed before us
with the brightness and beauty
of a shooting star

Our hearts are broken by the briefness
of her visit with us

She has climbed onto our Father God's lap
and is whispering to him our secrets
with sweet confidence
Speak to her in your hearts
the only language she will ever know is love

But how did this all begin? About a year before, my friend Monique LeBlanc moved from North Vancouver to Saskatoon and began a blog to share her journey. I admired her courage in sharing her honest and playful writing. Within weeks of moving, Monique lost her son Hilary halfway through her pregnancy. I felt helpless to do anything but listen to her on the phone and pray. Monique continued to write with exquisite vulnerability. I wanted to offer a sacrifice to accompany her in her grief. For years, I had been scribbling in hidden journals, but now I pushed aside my fears and published my first blog post on "Just East of Crazy Land: Adventures in Parenting." Providentially, my blog would become a place for me to process my own grief in losing a baby the next year.

I found it very difficult to write about the experience of losing my daughter; the story of the tangled umbilical cord was too painful to explain in prose. Poetry, however, was a steam valve for my pent-up emotions and brought me relief. I could capture the feeling of the moment, whether the bittersweet pain at the sight of cherry blossoms by moonlight, so innocent and fragile, or the feeling of numbness and floating in a bubble while the rest of the world rushed on unaware.

Closer Than Ever

The grass is still green
on this side of the world
The sun still shines red
through my eyelids

It warms my upturned face
as the fall leaves fall
with delicate grace

Children still laugh
and the birds still fly
Flowers open and close

You're gone away
little one
but closer than ever

No longer does your heart
beat in my body
That quick little drum
has faded now

But now that you've gone
to be with the stars
you've ripped open my heart
exposed Heaven within and

I've found you
closer than ever
here in my soul

Sharing my poetry brought me comfort from all corners of the globe. No matter the time of day or night, there was a sympathetic response from one of my readers. Furthermore, grieving mothers said that my words gave expression to their feelings and helped them feel less alone. I came to have a sense of mission – that I was meant to reach out and comfort others in pain, especially bereaved parents.

If It's Only by Crying

If it's only by crying
that I can understand
the tears of others
then let me wear them like pearls

If it's only by losing hope
that I can bring it to others
then let it fly away

If it's only by breaking my heart
that it can become
big enough to hold everyone
break it

If it's only by my desolation
that I can walk the valley of grief
with others
then strip me bare

Let my fragility bring others courage
my vulnerability, strength

And from my emptiness
let Your light burst forth
and shine

Lead us through the valley of grief
because if we walk it together
it will bring us Home

My friend Julia, who had previously lost her son at 28 weeks, became an essential support in my grief journey. I had prayed for her after her loss, and now she bravely drew near me, even though she had just delivered her first rainbow baby, a girl, mere weeks before I lost Josephine. Julia gave me good advice on cherishing the few precious hours I had with my baby before burial and was so supportive in organizing the funeral and other special anniversaries. One day, she left a gift basket at my door. It was a Mother Mary Basket and was full of little comforting things like chocolates, bath salts, candles and tea. It also had some pamphlets and prayer cards about grief and faith, and a little wooden statue of an angel holding a baby.

Having my loss acknowledged this way was very moving because it helped me treat myself with gentleness. I struggled with feeling that my body had betrayed me by failing to keep my child safe, yet these loving gifts affirmed that it was still good and deserving of kindness. My mother once told me, when I was struggling with the first bitterly cold days after the loss of my fall baby, "Your baby was never cold; she went from your warmth to the warm heart of God." Rather than a tomb, my womb was a gate of Heaven.

Holy Saturday

Day of silence
Of exhausted aftermath
Of unbelief
Can it really have happened??

The strangeness of life continuing
Just as it had before
Yet—on the inside—
Earth-shatteringly different

Every mother who has lost a child
Knows this feeling
In the core of her soul

In her hollowed-out heart
In her empty aching arms

The day after death
For most of us
The long wait for reunion
For resurrection
Lasts a lifetime

One long Holy Saturday
Until death breaks the silence
And we hear our babies laugh

To endure this day
Stay close to the Mother
Of the One they pierced

No sorrow deeper
No love stronger
No patience more graceful
Than that of the one
Who spent Holy Saturday
Weeping tears of hope

I was now part of an amazing sisterhood of women who were surviving losing little ones. I helped make sure they received Mother Mary Baskets. Eventually, I thought of printing some of my grief poetry to include in the gift baskets, and I told my brother Monti about this when he was visiting from Hawaii.

"You're not going to just print your poems on paper and stick them in," he said. "You're going to publish them in a proper book!"

He handed me a hundred-dollar bill.

"Here. I'm investing in your project. You can do this!"

So, with his encouragement, I did. I published *unexpected blossoming: a journey of grief and hope* on Josephine's second anniversary. Doing this fulfilled my intense need to give her something for her birthday. We had a book release party at my house, attended by family, friends, and even my sweet midwives, who had already safely delivered my first rainbow baby, a little boy.

I continued to meet many baby-loss moms over the next few years. I remember one interaction very fondly. A woman was given my poetry book by a friend. She had miscarried about a year before and was weary of people asking if she wasn't "over it yet" or reassuring her that "it was for the best." She felt unsupported and alone in her grief, and at times almost questioned its validity. Her only visual memory of her tiny infant was of blood. I reassured her that her deep grief was a sign of her great motherly love for her child, who was just as much a child as the full-term baby I had lost, only smaller.

After reading my poetry, the woman told me about a special dream she had. She was in a flowery field, and a little girl with curly hair, just like her other children, came running toward her, smiling, and jumped into her arms. She was able to hug her daughter in heaven. This dream gave her so much comfort and hope. Now, instead of only mourning, she could also focus on looking forward to being together again.

When a child dies, your love for them continues beyond the grave, and so therefore does your relationship. What you need to figure out is what that will look like. There is nothing you can teach a child who is already in heaven, so perhaps that child is actually meant to teach you how to live better here on earth. Pour all the love you have for your child into creating something beautiful that will touch others' hearts; doing so brings healing and connection and fosters hope. When you allow your grief a place to exist, when you embody it in words, on a canvas, in photography or even in a garden, you allow your pain to be transformed into something beautiful. You affirm the goodness of life, even in the depths of your pain.

Dig deep into your core: What is your passion? What brings you joy? Lean into that. Do it for your child who didn't have the chance to discover their passions here on earth. Connect to them by connecting more deeply to yourself and to what makes you feel fully alive. Remember that Jesus said: "I came that they may have life, and have it abundantly" (John 10:10). Let your faith that your child truly lives give you the strength to seize joy. When you meet your child again, and they ask, "How did you spend your life after I left you?" what will you tell them?

I invite bereaved parents to share their stories with others. You never know how someone will be touched by your words, art or other creations. In 2021, my sister told me about a project called "Laments for a Modern World" by British Columbia soprano Ai Horton, who was doing her master's thesis in Holland. She was seeking grief poetry to turn into 17th-century-style songs of lament. I submitted several poems, and to my great surprise and delight, she chose my poem "Carry Me." It was the first thing I had written after Josephine died, capturing my raw grief as I cried in the shower. Ai worked with me to convey my experience of sorrow and did an incredible job rendering my simple words into a poignant song, accompanied by harp.[28]

If I hadn't shared those words I sobbed in the shower, they wouldn't now be set in gold by Ai's amazing soprano voice. Josephine, who never spoke, is now singing for all the world. Her song has given expression to the invisible pain of grieving someone who remains a part of us, even though almost no one else has met them. I am so proud of my tiny muse.

---

28 You can find Ai Horton's fascinating thesis on grief and lament at https://www.research-catalogue.net/view/1377562/1798193#tool-1946590, including the lyrics and recordings of the four songs in her project.

Every year on Josephine's birthday, September 30, my children and I plant fall flower bulbs, and every spring, our garden is more beautiful because of Josephine's flowers. We think of her daily when we see them. We bake her a birthday cake and sing for her; we get her a special ornament at Christmas or some art, like the little canvas of a solitary red-and-white mushroom that made me think of her. We continue to remember and to love. My uncle even had a real star named for her. We have the map; she is there, near the Big Dipper – Josephine Pilar – forever in the sky, forever shining down on us, forever turning our gazes to heaven.

Mom of ten ***Anna Eastland*** *is a Catholic convert and author of several books. Her next one,* Velvet Flame, *is a poetry book about rainbow babies and life after loss.*

Part 2

Pastoral Responses

Offering Slivers of Light

A Pastoral Response

Kathy Hendricks

Our pastor called one evening with a tender request. A woman in the parish had had a miscarriage, and her husband was concerned over her deep sadness and grief. To make matters worse, she only spoke Russian and therefore had few people to whom she could talk. Fr. Miller asked if my husband and I would be willing to accompany him on a home visit. When I demurred over the language barrier, he quickly reassured me. "You know the grief of a child's death," he noted. "Finding a way to communicate will come to you." He was right. Our one-year-old daughter, Jenny, had died a few months before. I knew well that words are inadequate at such a time. During our visit, I was able to communicate as one bereaved mother to another.

This long-ago experience still touches me deeply. Fr. Miller's response to the couple was sensitive, personal and kind. These three elements should be part of pastoral outreach during any experience of death and bereavement. When it comes to infant loss, they are essential. In addition, there is a need for both initial outreach as well as long-term support. The various circumstances around loss during pregnancy and after a child's birth call for a special kind of pastoral response. This chapter offers some suggestions for these tragic occurrences and ways to provide the kind of care that Fr. Miller exhibited to a couple in mourning.

Initial outreach

Recognize the importance of presence. Paying a visit to the home is a vital first step in providing pastoral care to parents who have lost a child. The first wave of grief, in which shock and pain surface, requires an urgent response on the part of parish ministers. Timing matters. The immediate aftermath of such a loss, however, does not call for theological explanations or a rush to "closure." Rather, it is a time to acknowledge the searing pain that besets the parents and others affected by the loss. As pastor and author Gerritt Dawson notes, "There are stages in prayer through which many of us pass in settling the weight of life's afflictions. Spiritual union with Jesus is the goal but is rarely accomplished in the beginning."[29] The importance of quiet presence cannot be overstated. Our willingness to simply listen as parents pour out their pain is one of the most tender forms of pastoral care.

Avoid platitudes. The death of a child draws out tough questions. One of the most challenging is about where God figures in the picture. Attempts to console with assurances of "God's plan" or "God's will" dismiss the very real pain and anguish of those devastated by a loss. It also paints a poor picture of God, one that is particularly out of place with a Christian view of compassion and mercy. Nowhere in the gospels do we read of Jesus shrugging

29 Gerritt Dawson, "Through a Glass Darkly," *Weavings*, Vol. XIII, no. 2.

off the suffering of others with a glib response. Instead, we see his willingness to suffer with and for us. In doing so, he shows us what it means to stand alongside those who suffer, willing to listen to them and to hold their pain in our own hearts.

Be mindful of the effects of trauma. Finding Jenny's lifeless body in her crib elicited from me a cry so deep and raw that it seemed like it came from somewhere far distant. Her death came after several months of watchful waiting as she underwent multiple surgeries to remedy an intestinal disease. While I was not aware of it at the time, I was undergoing a severe form of trauma.

Whether the death of an infant is prolonged or sudden, the effect on the parent is one of shock and indescribable anguish. This includes loss that occurs as a result of miscarriage or stillbirth. Providing care for a parent whose child has died requires particular sensitivity on the part of pastoral ministers. Parents are often confused about what to do next, and so a calm and caring response helps them through the initial stages of shock.

When such events occur without warning, there is little time to plan. Pastoral ministry involves flexibility in order to be responsive, as well as the stability of service that families find both comforting and dependable. It also requires great sensitivity to the parents' needs. The importance of protecting a family's privacy is paramount. While some want to be upfront about the circumstances of a child's death, others prefer to withhold information from others in the parish. Balancing all of these needs and concerns is a delicate task.

Draw upon those with similar experiences. Fr. Miller's assurance that I would find a way to communicate with the distraught mother was based on my own experience of infant loss. In addition, my husband's presence was a comfort to the father, who was grieving in his own way. Like-to-like ministry is a way to extend empathy and compassion during such a tender time. Who better understands what it is like to lose one's child than someone who has walked such a daunting and painful path? In drawing upon others who might accompany a pastoral minister during a home visit or help with other forms of outreach, be mindful of those who might overreach in their efforts to support the bereaved. While empathy is a precious ability to recognize another's pain, it is also vital to understand that each occurrence of infant death is unique. It is way too soon for a parent to be part of a support group, so those ministering in such circumstances must avoid sharing too much about their own experience.

Approach funerals and wakes with sensitivity. Most parishes manage the original aftermath of a tragic death by assisting family members with funeral arrangements. How well this is done, however, can vary widely. An excessive adherence to rules and norms leaves parents already devastated by the loss even more distressed and alienated from the institution that should be serving them with compassion and understanding. Sensitivity on the part of priests and lay ecclesial ministers goes a long way in assuring families of a genuine attentiveness to their suffering. Some families are so stricken by events that they are not sure what to do when it comes to planning a funeral. Others have specific requests for music, slide presentations or videos, storytelling and other tributes. Gentle guidance with a sensitivity to these requests, and yet remaining within parish or diocesan norms, ensures that wakes and funeral services provide comfort and consolation without becoming either impersonal or emotionally exhausting.

Long-term support

Provide ongoing presence. As the immediate shock of the loss begins to wane, other needs surface. Parishes with some form of grief ministry already have a structure for creating long-range plans for outreach and support. Miscarriage and infant death not only affect parents but also grandparents, siblings and other members of the family. As noted above, it is especially helpful to call upon those who have suffered similar losses and who understand the various needs that arise as time goes on. Not only do they have direct experience with this particular form of grief, but having worked enough with their own suffering, they are able to provide support without excessive self-reference. In addition to this direct ministry, pastoral leaders can remind parishioners of the importance of reaching out to parents and families after the funeral is over and the initial shock of the death starts to recede. This is often when loved ones are most vulnerable and in need of ongoing consolation.

Remain attentive during sensitive times of the year. When an infant loss occurs near the Christmas holidays, it poses an additional pastoral challenge. Cultural emphasis on merriment and cheer runs counter to the ongoing feeling of sadness and sorrow that envelops parents and other family members traumatized by grief and loss. Alternative worship, such as a "Blue Christmas" prayer service, provides opportunities to draw themes of Advent longing and Christmas hope into the experience of mourning. Ideas for these services are available online and can be expanded to include others who find the holidays a difficult time of year due to grief and loss.

Stay connected. One of the loneliest times for parents grieving the loss of a child is after the funeral and during the ensuing months. There is an assumption that the grieving process will somehow wrap up within six months to a year. For those who have had a miscarriage or stillbirth, the lack of any kind of memorial gathering or formal ministry makes the journey of grief all the harder to bear. Way too many parishes fail to acknowledge such loss in the same way as when a child has died. Remaining connected with the family might entail a grief support system composed of volunteers who are willing to communicate with the family through personal visits, phone calls, emails or handwritten notes. While published materials on grief and loss are overwhelming in the immediate aftermath of a death, these can provide additional support and consolation as the process of bereavement continues.

Offer opportunities for prayer. Draw upon liturgical solemnities and seasons to provide ways for grieving parents and families to join others who are grieving the loss of a child. All Saints' Day and All Souls' Day are especially appropriate for offering a special Mass or prayer service for infants who have died during the past year. A communal healing service is a powerful ritual in which to give expression to the suffering of grieving parents and the hope we have in the healing power of God's grace. Make use of this and other liturgies that bring families together to mourn as well as to pray for strength, guidance and grace. Consult the *Book of Blessings,* published by the United States Conference of Catholic Bishops, and online prayer resources for ideas about structuring the service. If space permits, planting a community garden for babies who died as a result of miscarriage can provide a space of remembrance for mothers and fathers who have no mementoes to remember their children.

The psalms offer a particularly rich way to give voice to the grief, anguish, confusion and dismay that accompany the loss of an infant. Incorporate these into prayer services, use them for *lectio divina* or send them to parents for their personal reflection. Psalms of sorrow and lament are especially meaningful in providing an outlet for one's pain. One or more of these psalms might be shared as part of pastoral visits or in email notes or other forms of communication with the family.

Emphasize hope. While infant loss brings terrible pain to parents and family members, our faith assures us of hope that lies beyond our deepest suffering: “For I am convinced that neither death, nor life, nor angels, nor rulers, nor things present, nor things to come, nor powers, nor height, nor depth, nor anything else in all creation, will be able to separate us from the love of God in Christ Jesus our Lord” (Romans 8:38-39). This beautiful passage reminds us of God’s eternal and merciful love. Draw upon this and other Scripture passages in the months that follow a death as a way to anchor the parents in hope. In doing so, pastoral care can offer slivers of light for those immersed in deep pain and the gentle reminder that life that will emerge once again.

Kathy Hendricks *is a spiritual director, author and speaker whose work in catechesis and pastoral ministry spans several decades. Her latest book is* Grace in the Wound: Finding Hope in Long-Term Grief *(Twenty-Third Publications).*

Walking Together through Listening

A Parish Priest's Perspective

Fr. Mark Gatto

A Church that listens

Is the Church a good listener? That has been the focus of the Catholic Church's worldwide Synod on Synodality (2021–2024). A synod is about the People of God walking together. On the way through this life, with its ups and downs, it is so important that we are able to walk together along the journey. One of the key elements needed for us to walk together is listening. Pope Francis highlighted this point when he stated in *Let Us Dream: The Path to a Better Future* (p. 84), "Synodality starts with hearing from the whole People of God. A Church that teaches must be firstly a Church that listens."

The challenge is to hear the quiet and often hidden voices in our communities: those on the margins and those who many times go unnoticed. Some of those quiet, often unheard voices in our parishes are those who experience miscarriage or infant loss.

So much suffering, grief and struggle remains hidden and unseen by others. As a parish priest through the years, I have often been surprised to discover great hurt within people that remained unknown to others. But after 33 years of priesthood, I am no longer surprised by the issues and hurts that people keep within, sometimes for all or most of their life. Miscarriage and infant loss often remain very private and receive no public acknowledgement.

Learning through listening

In his book on Christian community, *Life Together*, Dietrich Bonhoeffer wrote, "Just as love of God begins with listening to His Word, so the beginning of love for the brothers and sisters is learning to listen to them."

It was during my time as pastor at St. Matthew Parish in Oakville that the hidden cry of hurt in people who have experienced miscarriage or infant loss became very clear to me. It was through listening to one parishioner that I began to learn about this reality.

A parishioner who had experienced a miscarriage and was struggling to deal with this pain came to see me one day. Later on, she would tell me how difficult it was for her to take that step because she had spoken to another priest about it in the past, and the conversation had not gone well. She felt it was because he was not comfortable discussing the subject. Thankfully, eventually she found the courage to come to me and to be very vulnerable in sharing her experience and her grieving. She shared her struggles, pain and sense of isolation. She shared how she found it hard to pray afterward. As I listened to her, it became clear that some concrete action of the parish was needed. Together, along with our pastoral minister who had also experienced a miscarriage, we came up with the plan to hold a Mass of Remembrance.[30]

The Mass of Remembrance

We decided to call this a Mass of Remembrance (for pregnancy loss) and announced that it would be open to all parents or others who had lost children through miscarriage, stillbirth or perinatal death. We advertised this Mass in our bulletin, on a Facebook page and during Sunday Mass announcements. I was very uncertain as to what to expect or how many people would come out, but we forged ahead and scheduled the first Mass for October 20, 2011.

Each person who attended the Mass was offered a rose to symbolize the lost child they were remembering. After the prayers of petition, they were invited to bring the roses forward and place them in a vase before the altar.

Close to 50 roses were brought forward at this Mass

I heard so many different stories afterward while speaking to a number of those who took part. Some women had had a miscarriage up to 40 years earlier. It was the first time there had been any public acknowledgement or prayer for their child during those years. At least one who attended had gone through an abortion many years before. One family had recently experienced a miscarriage; the remains of the fetus were still kept at home, as they did not know what to do. We arranged a simple burial ceremony at the local cemetery for their child.

30 I would like to thank Kristin Zita and Joanne Montague, who were responsible for planning the Mass of Remembrance and who offered feedback on this chapter.

After this Mass, I became so aware of how isolated and alone in their sorrow many parents, grandparents and family members felt after this kind of devastating loss.

Following up

The Mass of Remembrance in 2011 was so meaningful and had such a positive impact, we decided to have more such Masses in the future. We would plan different ritual actions to take place each year. For example, those present would light a candle for each child being remembered. These Masses continued even after I left the parish.

Our listening also led us to find ways to make public these hidden cries in various ways within the regular life of the parish. One example was to include a petition in the Prayer of the Faithful at special times of year, such as Christmas, Mother's Day and Father's Day, to acknowledge parents who had experienced such a loss. We invited a speaker to come and address some of the questions people have after such a loss. These were the questions we heard from various people:

* Why didn't God hear my prayers?
* Is it okay to feel angry at God?
* How can my trust in God be restored?
* What does prayer mean now?

An act of listening within our parish allowed our parish to walk together in a better way because those who were impacted were truly heard.

"Let the little children come to me" (Mark 10:14)

The little children are the ones who were lost, but sometimes so are the grieving parents and family, who may feel helpless in the face of such a painful loss. Our church should be a community where people are able to go, trusting that they will be touched by the healing presence of Jesus. The first step is that we listen: that we open our hearts to realize the hurt that exists, often hidden within our community.

One of the hard things about listening to and caring for people dealing with such grief is our sense of helplessness. We cannot fix this in some simple way. Someone once said to me that what is so difficult about being with people in sickness and mourning is the sense of not being helpful. But he reminded me that Jesus was most helpful to us when he was helpless on the cross.

The Document for the Continental Stage (DCS) of the 2021–2024 Synod of Bishops features the title "Enlarge the Space of Your Tent." The tent refers to a space of communion, a place of participation and a foundation for mission. Some key words are "listening as openness to welcome."

This listening is rooted in the basic assumption that God listens to the People of God. This leads to the mission to "proclaim the face of a God who cares to the point of giving his own life" (DCS #11). This one mission of the Church arises from the common baptismal dignity. It requires participation and co-responsibility. From all continents there came an appeal "for Catholic women to be valued first and foremost as baptized and equal members of the People of God" (DCS #61). In particular, many women expressed that they "feel sadness because their lives are often not well understood" (DCS #61). When it comes to the reality of miscarriage and infant loss, it is often women who most directly feel this loss.

Our church and our clergy have the challenge of listening to women's voices. In our parish experience, it was one woman who had the courage to come forward and speak of her experience. It was then that two women, our pastoral minister and this parishioner, took on responsibility for organizing this Mass of Remembrance. It required me as the pastor to let go of control and allow those most directly impacted to lead the mission of the Church in this area. This is a model of the Church listening to women, then letting go of control and allowing them to lead the mission.

A Synodal Church is one in which we are walking together on the pilgrimage through life. This requires that we listen well, especially to those on the margins, to those who often go unheard. Each person needs to find their own way along this path of life, but if we share the journey, listening and walking together, then the way is much lighter.

The reality of miscarriage and infant loss is a challenge to our Church and our communities. We are called to learn to listen, to hear the often hidden and silent cries. Then we will be better able to walk together, to offer the care that each of us needs.

***Fr. Mark Gatto** served as Pastor at St. Matthew Parish in Oakville, Ontario, from 2006 to 2017. He is presently Pastor of St. Catherine of Siena Parish in Hamilton, Ontario, where two former parishes have been united and a new church is being built.*

Signposts

Creating and Celebrating Rituals for Those Grieving Miscarriage or Infant Loss

Fr. Bill Burke and Bernadette Gasslein

Dear colleagues in ministry, dear families, dear friends of those who are suffering the grief of miscarriages:

Thank you for your willingness to journey with the women and families of your community. What follows are some ritual resources that you can use with people going through this often invisible grief. Since the Catholic Church has no official rituals to use in these circumstances, beyond a couple of prayers for a "child who has died before Baptism" (*Order of Christian Funerals*, pp. 413–14), we have designed these for use in the home, in the hospital or in the church.

These resources are born of our own experience. Bernadette: I had two miscarriages and, despite my own professional and personal involvement in catechetical and liturgical ministry, I found few resources to assist at a time when I didn't have the spiritual or emotional energy to design rituals. Fr. Bill: As a celibate man, I was initially reluctant to create a spoken prayer to express the experience of such parents, particularly since every situation is different. In my 45 years of ordained ministry, I have seen people deal with this grief in various ways, and I am convinced now of the need for families to express this grief ritually. Both of us have learned that sometimes this grief is only addressed years after the loss.

If you choose to embark on this journey, know that it will be at times painful and always significant. To help you, here are some signposts born of our experiences.

Give the parents as much control as possible

Parents have experienced a huge loss, whether their child died in the womb at the age of six weeks – perhaps before the parents had told family or friends they were expecting – or was stillborn at six months, or died shortly after birth. Since this situation was totally out of their control, offering them options, so they can choose how to best ritualize their loss, is a blessing. These rituals may be significant events that they *can* control. That's why we invite you to share the options we've included here with families so they can choose among them. Don't just hand them the book and walk away. This is a time to gently engage them in a healing, prayerful conversation that may transform itself into the ritual.

If a couple or family wants you to prepare the ritual, these options will allow you, after having carefully listened to the mourners, to prepare a simple ritual. Unless you decide to have a Mass, there are no rubrics to dictate specifics. And even if you have a Mass, the rubrics of that liturgy are very generous.

Don't try to make this high church liturgy. It is simply a ritualized prayer/prayerful ritual that enables these bereaved parents to express their loss, sorrow, anxiety, pain, fear and/or anger to our God, in the presence of those family members and friends whom they want to include in this moment when they are seeking comfort.

Recognize emotions and own your own

A few months after ordination, Fr. Bill was called to the hospital in the middle of the night to pray with the parents and grandparents of a stillborn baby girl. Fr. Bill: I was stunned by my reaction when they brought me to the room and I saw a weeping mother holding a beautiful, perfectly formed little girl with almost translucent skin. I burst out crying. Fortunately, a wise nurse was present who ministered to all of us.

Parents who have lost a child before or at birth are experiencing powerful emotions. Of course there is intense grief, shock, anger, devastation.[31] Remember that from the very moment they discovered they were pregnant, they have invested hopes and dreams in this child. This child's death means the loss of both the child *and* the hopes and dreams that accompanied the pregnancy. Sometimes this is a woman's first miscarriage; sometimes it is the seventh or eighth. That is a lot of loss and a lot of grief.

Ministering to these families requires a truly compassionate person. If you are shocked, for instance, by the sight of a stillborn child, be prepared to admit your shock to yourself and trusted friends, and to the family, if it's appropriate. Our presence needs to be that of one who comforts, not one who is being comforted. Fr. Bill: Since that experience 45 years ago, I avoid actually looking at the child, and I tell families and medical staff why. If you don't feel anything, or can't understand why this loss is a big deal, find another person to minister to these people. Mechanical rubricism has no place here.

31 Elisabeth Kübler-Ross described five stages of grief: denial, anger, bargaining, depression and acceptance. These feelings can arise in any order but can be a useful reference point for pastoral ministers.

Our culture is reluctant to acknowledge this loss and, as others have noted, often discount it by comments such as "Oh well, you can have another" or "At least you weren't too far along." Such insensitive comments are often born out of not knowing what to say that would truly comfort. Don't add to people's sense of loss by such insensitivity. Saying nothing – just being there – is sometimes enough.

If you're a celibate male, be prepared to listen carefully to the stories of women's loss

Miscarriages happen in many ways, depending on the stage of pregnancy and fetal development. For some women, the experience of a miscarriage, particularly an early miscarriage, is like a heavy menstrual period. There will be little tissue that resembles anything like a fetus. In other instances, the fetus, if expelled intact, will look very much like a very tiny baby. Some women may need significant time to recover physically, particularly if they lost a lot of blood. Others may be physically fine quite quickly.

If you are an ordained person, people may share with you unedited details of this event. You can prepare for this by talking with female family members or close female friends about their own experiences of pregnancy and pregnancy loss. You may be shocked to learn how common a loss this is (15 to 20% of pregnancies end in miscarriages in the first eight weeks)[32] and how rarely it is acknowledged or discussed.

Support the dads as well as the moms

While it may be tempting to focus on the mother, remember that the dad has also lost a child. If the mother's loss is invisible (because of the stage of the pregnancy at which the miscarriage

32 Society of Obstetricians and Gynecologists of Canada, https://www.pregnancyinfo.ca/your-pregnancy/special-consideration/miscarriage.

occurred), the father's loss is even more invisible. He may be bewildered or angry as well as grieving. He might be afraid for his wife's well-being. Be sure that any prayers and rituals include him.

Every situation is different

Miscarriages can occur at any stage during the pregnancy, and the result can range from an unusual flow of blood to the formed body of a tiny baby. A "one-size-fits-all" ritual model won't work: every individual, couple and family member will be at a different point in their personal and faith journey.

The mom may be a single parent or newcomer without a strong support network; a couple may have married late and seen this pregnancy as their only chance at having a child; or this may be the most recent of several pregnancies in a large family. Another couple may have been repeatedly trying to have a child, and this may be one more of many miscarriages that have left them childless. Cultural expectations can also play into the situation. You will need to consider these as you plan a ritual.

One of the most significant factors is that, more than any other experience of loss, miscarriage is almost mandated by our culture to be a "private" grief that is unmarked by community recognition or involvement. Many parents do not want any form of ritual expression; others don't know if such thing is possible. Many do not even tell other family members if the miscarriage occurs before the pregnancy has been announced. Over the years, Fr. Bill has encountered so many different emotional reactions: faith pain – Why, God?; guilt –What did I do wrong? Was this my fault?; anger at what was seen as poor-quality medical care; frustration and depression, particularly when a woman has experienced many miscarriages; and intense loneliness that is relieved only when the loss is finally acknowledged.

In responding ritually, we must work with this wide range of emotions and situations.

How to speak of the child who has died

In 45 years of ordained ministry, Fr. Bill has learned that naming the child is very important. Fr. Bill: As my own niece taught me after the death of her 18-hour-old son, "Don't be afraid to say his name in our presence."

Listen to how parents speak of their deceased child. If they have named their child or had a naming ritual (see below), always use the baby's name and the appropriately gendered pronouns. Never use "it" to refer to the baby who has died.

Bernadette discovered that medical personnel will speak about the woman having a "spontaneous abortion." This is a medical term that can be very shocking when people are living this experience. It is not appropriate for use in a pastoral or liturgical context.

Do not use miscarriage as a reason to talk about abortion or pro-life issues, as someone once did when Bernadette had her first miscarriage. Parents are grieving precisely because they have lost a child. Talking about abortion in this context is abusive of the people who are already suffering. Never weaponize this grief-laden moment for right-to-life issues.

Creating rituals

The Order of Christian Funerals does not offer any rituals for parents who have lost a child before birth. It does, however, offer prayers to be used during a liturgy for children who have died before Baptism (Prayers and Texts in Particular Circumstances, p. 413, §13, 14, 15). These may be useful during these rituals.

We are offering you several options for rituals. The first is three different kinds of naming rituals. This will give you a chance to formally name the baby you have lost.

The second is the structure for a liturgy of lament. In the church's treasury of liturgical forms, lament is rarely used. In the Old Testament, it was used when people wanted to cry out to God in anger or reproach God for bad things happening to good people. We've lost the habit of praying or relating to God in this way, but it is a time-tested way of praying, especially in the face of things that we can't fathom or that are so painful we can't cope. "Complaining" to God is *honest* prayer that blows apart sanctimony and false piety. This honesty is good for us emotionally and spiritually.

In the Old Testament, laments had five parts:

* *an address to God* (such as a favourite name for God or a description of what God has done for us);
* *a complaint* (yes, a complaint to God! This was a very common way of praying in the Old Testament);
* *a confession or acknowledgement that we trust God* (usually because we've heard the word of God and are reminded of God's constancy and care, even in the worst events of our lives; that's why we've included scripture passages here);
* *petitions:* we're complaining and asking God for what we need, almost in the same breath;
* *thanksgiving:* we thank God for what God has done for us in the past that reminds us of God's faithfulness and in anticipation that God will continue to be with us in all things in the future.

We've provided a number of samples of each of these parts to prompt your own prayer or to use as they are.

A final section offers more formal options; these might be used by a parish in planning an annual Mass for families who have lost a child to miscarriage or stillbirth.

I. Naming your baby and commending him/her to God

Even those parents who say they haven't decided on a name for their baby start thinking about what to call their little one early in their pregnancy. Particularly if they know the sex of their child, they often start talking to the baby by name. The little one may already have heard their name for weeks or months. Naming your child makes his or her presence and absence real.

If the child's body is present, your local funeral director will help you arrange for his or her burial.

You may want to consider eventually doing something like what Fr. Bill's niece did when her baby died when he was 18 hours old: she had Christmas tree ornaments made with his picture on it. You may simply want to inscribe your baby's name on the ornament.

A simple ritual

This may take place at the home or hospital. If the pregnancy ended before the sex of the child could be determined, the parents can choose a favourite saint, traditional family name or the name of someone they wish to honour. When they and their child are united in the life to come, if they got it wrong, they will have a good story to share.

A. If there are no remains present

All who are gathered who are Catholic may make the Sign of the Cross. Then the parents say,

"Child of our love, we entrust you to the Holy One who knew you from before the moment you came into being. In our family, we will always remember your brief time among us and call you by this name: ____________________."

Then, all together, or each person present individually can say, "N. ________________, we will love you forever."

They may close by saying together the Our Father.

B. If there are remains present

All who are gathered who are Catholic may make the Sign of the Cross. Then the parents or the presider touch the urn or coffin, and pray, "God, we entrust into your love this little one whom we ask you to name N. ____________ for all eternity. Grant that when we meet again in the life to come, we will be united in your love."

Then, all together, or each person present individually can say, "N. ________________, we will love you forever."

They may close by saying together the Our Father.

A more formal naming and commendation ritual

This could take place at home or at church. The presider could be a family member, such as a grandparent, aunt or uncle, dear friend, parish priest, or the deacon and/or his wife, where appropriate.

Presider: In the name of the Father, + and of the Son, and of the Holy Spirit.

All: Amen.

Presider: My friends, in the face of death, especially the death of an infant, we experience a grief beyond words. Today, we gather in faith to experience the compassion of the God who, in Jesus, has conquered death and opened heaven to all.

(For a stillborn child whose body is present, if the child has already been named, this section is omitted.)

We gather today to commend this child to God's embrace. And we begin by naming this child.

Presider asks the parents:
What name do you give your child?
(Parents respond)

Presider: In the name of this Christian community, I sign N. __________ with the Sign of the Cross, and I invite those present to do the same.

In case of miscarriage, the presider asks,
By what name would you have wanted your child to be known among God's children?
Why were you drawn to this name?
(Parents respond)
(The signing is omitted.)

Reading of the Gospel

Matthew 11:28
"Come to me, all you that are weary and are carrying heavy burdens, and I will give you rest."
or
Mark 10:13-16
People were bringing little children to Jesus in order that he might touch them; and the disciples spoke sternly to them. But when Jesus saw this, he was indignant and said to them, "Let the little children come to me; do not stop them; for it is to such as these that the kingdom of God belongs. Truly I tell you, whoever does not receive the kingdom of God as a little child will never

enter it." And he took them up in his arms, laid his hands on them, and blessed them.

Prayer

Presider: Trusting in Jesus, the loving Saviour,
who gathered children into his arms
and blessed the little ones,
we now commend this infant [N.]
 to that same embrace of love,
in the hope that he (she) will rejoice
and be happy in the presence of Christ.

All pray in silence.

Lord Jesus,
lovingly receive this little child;
bless him (her)
and take him (her) to your Father.
We ask this in hope,
for you live and reign for ever and ever.

All: Amen.

(*Order of Christian Funerals,* §549)

The Lord's Prayer

Presider: United with our heavenly Father who grieves with all his children, we pray:

All: Our Father …

Prayer of Commendation

Presider: Tender Shepherd of the flock,
N. now lies cradled in your love.
Soothe the hearts of his (her) parents
and bring peace to their lives.

All: Amen.

(*Order of Christian Funerals*, §551)

Sign of Peace

Presider: Let us offer each other a sign of Christ's peace.

Blessing

Presider: May the love of God and the peace of the Lord Jesus Christ bless and console us and gently wipe every tear from our eyes, in the name of the Father, + and of the Son, and of the Holy Spirit.
All: Amen.

Presider: Let us go in the peace of Christ.
All: Thanks be to God.

Calling on the Saints

In the Catholic tradition, we refer to the date of someone's death as their birthday into eternity. Be sure to record the day of your child's death and look in the liturgical calendar (get your pastor to help you) to see which saint's feast day is celebrated on that day. Entrust your child to the care of that saint whose feast day he or she now shares.

II. Lament your loss

You may want to pray this as a family or alone. If it comforts you, light a candle. You may want to sit quietly for a while or listen to some music that brings you comfort or calm.

1. Address to God

Here are some of the ways you can speak to God.

☐ God,

☐ God, who loves us with a mother's love,

☐ God, who loves us as a father loves his children,

☐ God, who is with us no matter what happens,

☐ God, who is close to the broken-hearted,

☐ God of tenderness and compassion,

☐ God, who has loved us from when we were in our mother's womb,

☐ God, who promised to be with us,

☐ God of life,

☐ ______________________ [my favourite name for God]

2. *Complaint*

What is wrong? If any of these feels familiar, it may help you express your complaint. Or you can use these as a starting point to write or speak your own complaint to God,

It may seem very strange to pray to God this way. But in fact, by pouring out our complaints to God, we draw closer to God and God to us. God will not be angry at you for expressing your complaint. In fact, in the passages from the Bible that are included after this section, you will find one that contains Jesus' most profound complaint: "My God, my God, why have you forsaken me?" as well as Psalm 22, from which Jesus borrowed those words for his complaint.

Parents

☐ The baby we longed for has died in my womb … My heart is broken.

☐ We asked for a child, and now that child is dead … My husband can't bear to talk about it. I feel so alone.

☐ You are the God of life, and my child has died without knowing life … Why did you let this happen, God? Why?

☐ Why are you silent? Why didn't you stop my baby from dying? Why, God, why?

☐ Why me, God? Everyone else seems to get pregnant so easily and have babies so easily. This is my ________ miscarriage. Why this again? Why do well-meaning friends tell me I can always have another? It hasn't worked that way!

☐ I feel so alone. Everyone else has kids, and everyone else seems so happy. If I tell them, they just walk away. They don't know what to say.

☐ I feel so alone. My wife has been crying and I can't console her. I don't know what to do, God.

☐ God, my baby died decades ago. I didn't realize how much I missed that child until now. How could you have let that happen? I wish I had named my child. How will I know him/her?

Siblings

☐ My mom and dad are sad. My mom was going to have a baby, but the baby died. They try to hide their tears from me, but I can see that my mom is crying. Why do you let babies die, God? When will we get another baby?

☐ My mom and dad are sad. My mom was going to have a baby, but the baby died. I feel really sad, too, God.

☐ God, I'm mad at you. I wanted a baby brother or sister, and now everyone is sad. Why did the baby die?

Grandparents

☐ At our wedding, the priest prayed, "May you see your children's children." Now our grandchild is dead. Why did you take back your blessing, God?

3. Confession of Trust

This step is difficult. In some ways, it's like the trust walk exercise that many of us have done in team-building exercises. Dare we risk letting ourselves fall into the love of our God … our spouse … our kids … our family … when it feels like life has betrayed us? Will God – our beloved – our family – our friends – catch us? Here are some scripture passages to ponder. Pick one or two and read them aloud.

Jeremiah 29:11

For surely I know the plans I have for you, says the LORD,
plans for your welfare and not for harm,
to give you a future with hope.

Psalm 22:1-5

My God, my God, why have you forsaken me?
Why are you so far from helping me, from the words of my groaning?
O my God, I cry by day, but you do not answer; and by night, but find no rest.
Yet you are holy, enthroned on the praises of Israel.
In you our ancestors trusted; they trusted, and you delivered them.
To you they cried, and were saved; in you they trusted, and were not put to shame.

Psalm 139:14-16

I praise you, for I am fearfully and wonderfully made.
Wonderful are your works; that I know very well.
My frame was not hidden from you,
when I was being made in secret, intricately woven in the depths of the earth.
Your eyes beheld my unformed substance.

Isaiah 25:6-8a

On this mountain the LORD of hosts will make for all peoples a feast of rich food, a feast of well-aged wines, of rich food filled with marrow, of well-aged wines strained clear.
And he will destroy on this mountain the shroud that is cast over all peoples . . .;
he will swallow up death forever.
Then the Lord GOD will wipe away the tears from all faces.

Isaiah 43:1-2, 4a

But now thus says the LORD, he who created you. . .:
Do not fear, for I have redeemed you; I have called you by name, you are mine.
When you pass through the waters, I will be with you; and through the rivers, they shall not overwhelm you;
when you walk through fire you shall not be burned,
and the flame shall not consume you.
Because you are precious in my sight, and honoured,
and I love you.

Isaiah 49:15

Can a woman forget her nursing-child,
or show no compassion for the child of her womb?
Even these may forget, yet I will not forget you.

Isaiah 54:10

For the mountains may depart and the hills be removed,
but my steadfast love shall not depart from you,
and my covenant of peace shall not be removed,
says the LORD, who has compassion on you.

Lamentations 3:17-18, 19-23, 25-26

My soul is bereft of peace;
I have forgotten what happiness is;
so I say, "Gone is my glory, and all that I had hoped for from the LORD." …
My soul continually thinks of it and is bowed down within me.
But this I call to mind, and therefore I have hope:
The steadfast love of the LORD never ceases, his mercies never come to an end;
they are new every morning; great is your faithfulness.
The LORD is good to those who wait for him,
to the soul that seeks him.
It is good that one should wait quietly for the salvation of the LORD.

John 6:39

"And this is the will of him who sent me, that I should lose nothing of all that he has given me, but raise it up on the last day."

Matthew 5:4

"Blessed are those who mourn, for they will be comforted."

Matthew 11:28

"Come to me, all you that are weary and are carrying heavy burdens, and I will give you rest."

Mark 10:13-16

People were bringing little children to Jesus in order that he might touch them; and the disciples spoke sternly to them. But when Jesus saw this, he was indignant and said to them, "Let the little children come to me; do not stop them; for it is to such as these that the kingdom of God belongs. Truly I tell you, whoever does not receive the kingdom of God as a little child will never enter it." And he took them up in his arms, laid his hands on them, and blessed them.

Mark 15:33-34

When it was noon, darkness came over the whole land until three in the afternoon. At three o'clock Jesus cried out with a loud voice, "Eloi, Eloi, lema sabachthani?" which means, "My God, my God, why have you forsaken me?"

John 3:16-17

"For God so loved the world that he gave his only Son, so that everyone who believes in him may not perish but may have eternal life. Indeed, God did not send the Son into the world to condemn the world, but in order that the world might be saved through him."

John 11:21-27

Martha said to Jesus, "Lord, if you had been here, my brother would not have died. But even now I know that God will give you whatever you ask of him." Jesus said to her, "Your brother will rise again." Martha said to him, "I know that he will rise again in the resurrection on the last day." Jesus said to her, "I am the resurrection and the life. Those who believe in me, even though they die, will live, and everyone who lives and believes in me will never die. Do you believe this?" She said to him, "Yes, Lord, I believe that you are the Messiah, the Son of God, the one coming into the world."

2 Corinthians 1:3b-4a

Blessed be the God and Father of our Lord Jesus Christ, the Father of mercies and the God of all consolation, who consoles us in all our affliction, so that we may be able to console those who are in any affliction with the consolation with which we ourselves are consoled by God.

1 Thessalonians 4:13-14, 18

But we do not want you to be uninformed, brothers and sisters, about those who have died, so that you may not grieve as others do who have no hope. For since we believe that Jesus died and rose again, even so, through Jesus, God will bring with him those who have died. Therefore encourage one another with these words.

Revelation 21:1a, 3-5a

Then I saw a new heaven and a new earth; for the first heaven and the first earth had passed away, and the sea was no more.
And I heard a loud voice from the throne saying,
"See, the home of God is among mortals.
He will dwell with them;
they will be his peoples,
and God himself will be with them;
he will wipe every tear from their eyes.
Death will be no more;
mourning and crying and pain will be no more,
for the first things have passed away."
And the one who was seated on the throne said,
"See, I am making all things new." Also he said,
"Write this, for these words are trustworthy and true."

After you have pondered a passage from the Bible, take some time to think about taking the step to trusting God. Here are some words to express our trust:

- ☐ Into your hands, O Lord, I commend my spirit.
- ☐ Protect me, O God, for in you I take refuge.
- ☐ God, I put my life/our lives in your hands.
- ☐ God, it's very hard for me to trust you and my future right now. But I know you love me/us, and I know that you will heal my body and my/our spirit(s).
- ☐ God, I give you my family and my own self. I give you our precious baby who died. I know that you will change our sorrow to joy.

Siblings

- ☐ God, even though it's hard, I trust that you will take care of me, my mommy and daddy, and our baby who died.

Grandparents

- ☐ God, you have seen us through many difficulties and challenges. We know that you will help us again.

4. Petition

Now we ask God for what we need, and we pray for others as well. You can certainly ask for as many of these as you wish – and feel free to add other requests.

- ☐ Turn my sadness to joy.
- ☐ Take away my depression.
- ☐ Heal my body and my spirit.
- ☐ Help me to get pregnant again.
- ☐ Heal the broken-hearted.
- ☐ Protect all mothers who are pregnant.

- ☐ Sustain those who have difficult pregnancies.
- ☐ Comfort those whose babies will die today.
- ☐ Give wisdom and understanding to the doctors and nurses who helped me.
- ☐ Help pregnant women who live in war-torn countries or who have no food for themselves or their children.
- ☐ ____
  (Something I want to pray for)

5. *Thanksgiving*

Now we come to the last part of this ritual: praise and thanksgiving to God.

> God of life, I/we know you are faithful, and that you never abandon your creation.
> I /we know that you love us so much that you became human just as we are;
> your Son, Jesus, was conceived and grew in Mary's womb,
> and was born and died, just as we are born and die.
> You loved Jesus and you love each one of us from all eternity to the end of time and beyond.
> You continue to love all creation through your Holy Spirit,
> who raises up new life and gives us the hope that death does not have the final word in our lives,
> even when all seems dark.
> We thank you for your presence among us, today and every day,
> and ask you to help us to heal and to find happiness in the days ahead.
> We make this prayer in Jesus' name. Amen.

III. Praying as a parish

1. Book of Life

If your parish has a book of life where people can write the names of loved ones who have died during the last year, be sure to invite families to write the names of children who have died through miscarriage.

2. A Mass on or around All Souls' Day (November 2), December 20 or 21 (the longest day), the Feast of St. Catherine of Sweden (March 24), or in October, Pregnancy and Infant Loss Awareness Month

We take our cue from two popular celebrations. The first is the feast of All Souls on November 2. Many parishes hold a special Mass that day to honour all those of the parish who have died in the last year. Their names are read aloud, and a family member lights a candle for them. Perhaps a moment could be set aside at this time to remember babies who died in the womb or soon after birth, and to light a candle in their memory. In Fr. Bill's parish, these candles are lit for all Sunday masses until the beginning of Advent.

A second is the celebration of "the Longest Night," also known as "Blue Christmas." This event developed in early-21st-century Christian churches and is held on December 20 or 21 or another appropriate day in Advent. It recognizes that the Christmas holiday is often especially painful for those who have lost loved ones. The community gathers to support these people with prayer, scripture, poetry and song.

St. Catherine of Sweden is the patron saint of those who have experienced miscarriages. We invite you to dedicate a day near her feast, March 24, as the annual liturgical celebration for those who have had a miscarriage. It could be a Mass or a service of the Word incorporating song and ritual similar to "the Longest Night." If the date falls in Holy Week, schedule it for another time during the year.

October is Pregnancy and Infant Loss Awareness Month. You might want to set a date for an annual celebration during this month.

While such a celebration would be a communal one, its format would provide a comfortable level of anonymity or privacy. For a service of the Word, you can draw on some of the ideas in parts I and II.

3. Mass on the Feast of St. Catherine of Sweden

Introduction

Presider: Two traditions in our church combine today (this evening). The first is the tradition of referring to the date of the death of a saint as the saint's *dies natalis*, that is, the day of their birth. The custom dates back to the earliest days of the Church, when Christians would gather on the anniversary of the martyrdom of the saint to celebrate it as the day they were born into heaven.

The second tradition is that of designating certain saints as patronal saints who are associated with particular needs or causes (perhaps the most famous is St. Anthony, who is the patron of lost items). Today, we gather under the patronage of St. Catherine of Sweden. St. Catherine, who gave her life in service to the poor, had a special care for women who experienced difficult pregnancies and, even more especially, women who had miscarriages. St. Catherine died on March 24, so in keeping with the custom of *dies natalis*, her feast day is March 24, the anniversary of her birth into heaven. And so, we gather to commemorate the *dies natalis* of all the precious children who went home to God this past year and to pray that their parents and families experience the tender and loving embrace of God.

The celebration of Eucharist now begins and continues until after the Homily.

Ritual

In each seat, place small "dies natalis" cards and pencils. Participants who wish to do so may enter the date of their child's death along with the child's name or names they had thought about.

Blessing of roses and candles

Place a table on which you have one or several (depending on the size of your parish) vases of red roses and trays of candles in a prominent place in front of the altar. Red roses remind us that heaven is our destiny, a homeland opened by the blood and love of Christ. Candles call us to celebrate the light of Christ in our world and to be children of the light.

Prayer

O loving God, your own Son knew the pain of loss as he wept at the death of his friend Lazarus. Send your gift of his healing compassion upon us today to strengthen our faith that in Christ, life is changed, not ended. Nourish our hope that one day we shall all be together again in heaven, our true homeland. Bless these roses as a reminder of your love for us and our love for our child[ren] lost to miscarriage. Bless these candles as a sign of Christ's light that sustains us even in the darkest of our nights. We ask this through Christ our Lord.
All: Amen.

Invite each family to come forward in procession to place their "dies natalis" card in a basket and receive a rose and a candle to take home at the end of the celebration.

After all have returned to their places, the liturgy continues as usual.

Following the prayer after communion, the presider invites all to rise, then says the following prayer of commendation:

Presider: Tender Shepherd of the flock,
N. now lies cradled in your love.*
Soothe the hearts of his (her) parents
and bring peace to their lives.
Enlighten their faith
and give hope to their hearts.

Loving God,
grant mercy to your entire family in this time of suffering.
Comfort us with the hope that this child [N.]
lives with you and your Son, Jesus Christ,
and the Holy Spirit,
for ever and ever.
All: Amen.
(*Order of Christian Funerals,* §551; *use "these children" (and adapt the subsequent verbs and pronouns) if it's a Mass for many babies who have died)

Song of the Angels: For a musical setting, see *Catholic Book of Worship III*, 10c.

The liturgy concludes with this blessing:
Presider: May the God of all consolation
bring you* comfort and peace,
in the name of the Father, + and of the Son,
and of the Holy Spirit.
All: Amen.
(Order of Christian Funerals, §553; *if a lay minister is presiding, replace "you" with "us" and sign yourself (not those gathered) with the Sign of the Cross)

Fr. Bill Burke, *a priest of the Diocese of Antigonish, Nova Scotia, is a former director of the National Liturgy Office of the Canadian Conference of Catholic Bishops. He is currently pastor of St. Marguerite Bourgeoys Parish, Sydney, and St. Anne's Church, Membertou.*

Bernadette Gasslein *is a liturgist, catechist, author and musician who lives in Edmonton, Alberta. Currently she is the editor of* Worship, *the flagship publication of the Liturgical Movement, published by Liturgical Press, Collegeville, Minnesota.*

Connecting, Sharing, Supporting

Creating a Diocesan Miscarriage Awareness Committee

Shannon Granger

Baby number 3 was on the way. Everything was going along normally. I went to a monthly check-up in December and heard the best sound in the world… our baby's heartbeat. A month later, still feeling normal, I went to my January check-up, but there was no heartbeat this time. An ultrasound would confirm that our baby was no longer living. I've shared our story many times before, but the good and beautiful that came from our loss has not been told in its entirety before now.

My husband, Dan, and I experienced great support, largely due to our openness. Everyone around us knew we were expecting, so it was much easier to share the loss. Our parish priest at the time was wonderfully compassionate but didn't know how to support us. When I asked for a simple liturgy to ritualize our grief, he said he would do whatever sort of service we wanted, but he couldn't really direct us as he had never celebrated a life of a miscarried baby before. This pastor had been a priest for nearly 40 years! I know now that a Eucharistic celebration would have been so much better, but at the time a Liturgy of the Word was what I planned. I gathered resources from all sorts of materials and created a simple but meaningful-to-me liturgy. On the eve of a great winter storm, we gathered a small group of family and friends in the chapel of our church.

Over the weeks and months that followed, the support from friends who had experienced miscarriages themselves was wonderful. Time and tears were great healers. Over the next while, I couldn't shake the experience of the priest not knowing what to offer us. Counsel and prayer most certainly were needed, but I wondered how others managed if they didn't have an open and responsive priest, as we did. I could prepare a liturgy because I have ministry training, but so many people just suffer in silence because we haven't created a space to allow them to share the joy of being pregnant and, in the event of a miscarriage, the same space to grieve. We as a Church are pro-life, but this is an area where we were falling short.

As conversations moved from sadness to joy (and trepidation) as we were pregnant again, I started conversations with the diocese where we lived (Saskatoon), suggesting that education was needed for the leadership. With the full backing of the diocesan ministry coordinator, a committee was struck. We bumbled through for quite a while, unsure of our direction, as we needed to share our stories first. Most of the members had experienced at least one miscarriage, and those who hadn't were able to share their tangential experiences. Everyone had been touched by the loss of a miscarried baby.

Our group started with my diocesan contact, then we built the group together. I was the first member. Two parish nurses joined us, then the hospital chaplain, and a dear couple who were our (my and Dan's) greatest supports. The group, called the diocesan Miscarriage Awareness Committee, changed over the few years we were active as jobs changed – for example, a new diocesan representative was appointed – but a wonderful core group of faithful folks did great work. Our goal was to shine a light on the fact that families suffer, most often in silence, when they miscarry: we wanted to offer tools and resources to those in positions of leadership and support so they could better serve their communities.

We worked with the communications staff at the diocese and started building the website[33] in preparation for the fall meeting of the diocesan leadership. At the fall administration day, we were given a short time slot to share with the clergy and lay leadership. We shared our personal stories, statistics, some do's and don'ts, as well as the resources we had accumulated so far. I knew we were on the right track when a priest emailed me a few weeks later, saying, "Thank you. I used the resources."

To continue the awareness campaign in the diocese, we prepared bulletin announcements and prayer intentions for Mass to acknowledge Pregnancy and Infant Loss Remembrance Day, observed every October 15. As we continued moving along in our advocacy, we decided that even though we were not a support group, we could offer support in a simple way through a book. We found a resource we liked that contained reflections and scripture and was also a journal. With financial support from the Bishop's Appeal, we purchased and distributed books to anyone who called.

33 See https://rcdos.ca/ministries-services/marriage-and-family-life/miscarriage-awareness.

A local funeral home and grief centre was a great support as well; it offered space to meet, provided printing services, and included us in their annual prayer service for preborn and infant loss. They also will inter under their large monument the remains of miscarried babies. Families may also wish to have their baby acknowledged on the monument itself.

We organized a workshop called "1 in 4," referring to the number of babies lost through miscarriage. We had speakers, offered our stories and allowed time for others to share their stories. This was a time for families to connect and support each other.

Our most recent project that we worked on as a committee was the Tree of Hope. We wanted a place for people to go and pray, to be and remember. We had so much support: Queen's House Retreat and Renewal Centre in Saskatoon donated the space and found a local nursery to donate a tree. A family donated signs to mark the path to the Tree of Hope. The grounds at Queen's House are beautiful: it overlooks the river and is peaceful and serene. We had a lovely blessing of the tree with families gathered to remember their little one, to pray and find peace, if only for a moment.

Shannon Granger *is a wife, mother and parish staffer.*

Appendix 1

Praying in the Midst of Grieving

When heartbreak strikes, sometimes the last thing we feel like doing is praying. Sometimes there are no words to express the pain, the loss, the numbness. Thankfully, prayer doesn't always require words. At times of loss, when we are in the depths, tears, primal cries, exercise, art, cooking, cleaning, silence and more can all be wordless prayers that reach the heart of God.

But prayers with words that you can return to in time of need are a gift. This section contains prayers and Scripture passages that might speak to you. You may choose to write your own, from your own experience and faith. Or you may want to pray traditional prayers that get you through the day (or night): the Rosary, the Hail Mary, the Guardian Angel prayer.

Whatever form your prayer takes, our faith reminds us that our God is with us, sharing our heartache and offering us the hope of resurrection.

Prayer after a Miscarriage

Merciful God,

The loss of my baby weighs heavily on me.
I am overcome with grief and pain.
Unlike other experiences of death,
I have no photos or other memorabilia
to provide comfort.
Hold me to the hope that my baby rests
now with you,
and that, in time, some form of life
will arise in my family and in me.

With trust in your loving care, I pray.

Amen.

Prayer for a Resilient Spirit

God of Mercy and Love,

Anchor me in your Spirit.
When the winds of change set me adrift,
tether me to the hope I have in your
everlasting presence.
When storms of heartbreak and loss rain
down upon me, give me shelter.
When fatigue and discouragement pull me
into an undertow of despair,
buoy me with gentle reminders
of your ever-present grace.
May I find, through you, the strength
and stamina I need to ride the waves
of loss.
In doing so, may I also find joy in sailing
with your Spirit as I care for myself
and the people I love.

Amen.

Scripture verses for meditation and comfort

I keep the Lord always before me;
  because he is at my right hand, I shall not be moved.
(Psalm 16:8)

Even though I walk through the darkest valley,
  I fear no evil;
for you are with me;
  your rod and your staff—
  they comfort me.
(Psalm 23:4)

God is my refuge and strength,
  a very present help in trouble.
(Psalm 46:1)

When I am afraid,
  I put my trust in you.
In God, whose word I praise,
  in God I trust; I am not afraid.
(Psalm 56:3-4)

O give thanks to the Lord, for he is good;
  his steadfast love endures for ever!
(Psalm 118:1)

Come to me, all you that are weary and are carrying heavy burdens, and I will give you rest.
(Matthew 11:28)

Blessed are those who mourn, for they will be comforted.
(Matthew 5:5)

Appendix 2

Initiatives and Resources

Initiatives

- **Canadian Hospice Palliative Care Association**: The association's Grief and Bereavement Resource Repository contains a wide range of online resources for those who are grieving, including kids and teens.

https://www.chpca.ca/resource/grief-and-bereavement-resource-repository/

- **Catholic Moms**: This not-for-profit organization ministers to Catholic moms.

https://www.catholicmomsgroup.com

- **The Compassionate Friends**: This self-help organization offers friendship, understanding and hope to bereaved families after a child dies.

https://www.compassionatefriends.org/mission-statement/

- **Diocese of Saskatoon Miscarriage Awareness web page**: This web page offers a range of resources, including a pamphlet on grieving the child I never knew, a naming ceremony, and more.

https://rcdos.ca/ministries-services/marriage-and-family-life/miscarriage-awareness/

- **Elizabeth Ministry**: Elizabeth Ministry offers support after loss of a child during pregnancy, at birth, in infancy or in toddlerhood. Elizabeth Ministers journey with, support and pray for those who have experienced such a loss.

https://olos.ca/ministries/elizabeth-ministry/

- **Little Light of Heaven**: This website offers support to bereaved families after the loss of a child – during pregnancy, at birth, in infancy or as a toddler.

https://littlelightofheaven.com

- **Mother Mary Baskets**: Mother Mary Baskets offer spiritual and practical comfort resources for newly bereaved parents.

spicefertilitycare@gmail.com

- **Morning Light Ministry**: This is a Catholic ministry for bereaved mothers and bereaved fathers who have experienced the death of their baby through ectopic pregnancy, miscarriage, stillbirth or infant death up to one year old.

http://www.morninglightministry.org

- **My Grief.ca (Canadian Virtual Hospice)**: This confidential and free site helps the bereaved understand and move through their grief at their own pace.

https://www.mygrief.ca

- **Precious Angel Gowns**: This volunteer-run organization offers gowns and angel wraps at no charge to families that have suffered the loss of a beloved baby.

https://preciousangelgowns.com/donate-a-gown/

• **Share**: Pregnancy and Loss Support: Share provides support for those who have experienced perinatal loss.

https://nationalshare.org/sharing-magazine/

• **Sunnybrook Pregnancy and Infant Loss Network**: This network offers support to those who are experiencing the loss of a pregnancy or the death of a baby.

https://pailnetwork.sunnybrook.ca/about-us/who-we-are/

• **Tiny Shroud Ministry**: This parish ministry in Toronto knits blankets and hats for infants from 1 lb. to newborn sizes for hospitals and funeral homes.

TinyShroudMinistry@gmail.com or
stedwardtheconfessorno@archtoronto.org

• **Unexpectingbook.com**: This website, based on Rachel Lewis's book *Unexpecting: Real Talk on Pregnancy Loss*, features a blog and a discussion group.

Resources

Canadian Conference of Catholic Bishops, *Burying the Dead, Grieving Well: A Guide for Catholics on Bodily Disposition and Grief* (CCCB, 2022); see especially pages 27 and 28.

Paula D'Arcy, *When People Grieve: Guidance for Grievers and the Friends Who Care* (Crossroad, 2005).

Karen Edmisten, *After Miscarriage: A Catholic Woman's Companion to Healing and Hope* (Servant Books, 2012).

Carole M. Eipers, *How to Talk to Children about Death* (Twenty-Third Publications, 2019).

Laura Kelly Fanucci and Franco David Fanucci, *Grieving Together: A Couple's Journey through Miscarriage* (Our Sunday Visitor, 2018).

Kathy Hendricks, *Grace in the Wound: Finding Hope in Long-Term Grief* (Twenty-Third Publications, 2023).

Heidi Indahl, *Blessed Is the Fruit of Thy Womb: Rosary Reflections on Miscarriage, Stillbirth and Infant Loss* (Our Sunday Visitor, 2019).

Anne Marie S. Mahoney, *A New Parish Guide to Grief Ministry: Creative Ways to Implement a Program of Healing and Growth* (Twenty-Third Publications, 2023).

Patrick O'Hearn and Bryan Feger, with Kelly and Ryan Breaux of Red Bird Ministries, *The Grief of Dads: Support and Hope for Catholic Fathers Navigating Child Loss* (Ave Maria Press, 2023).

Joyce Rupp, *May You Find Comfort: A Blessing for Times of Grieving* (Ave Maria Press, 2010).

Breda Theakston, *Miscarriage: Caring for Yourself and Others* (Novalis, 2021).

United States Conference of Catholic Bishops, "Blessing of Parents after a Miscarriage or Stillbirth," https://www.usccb.org/prayers/blessing-parents-after-miscarriage-or-stillbirth.

My Grieving Journey Book (for children) (Paulist Press, 2002).